Praise for Pay Yourself First

Excellent—A Must-Read!

"How do we make Black America better? By under-standing that at the bottom of all of our struggle, must be the struggle for economic independence. Jesse Brown reminds us that we gain financial suc-cess and security when we pay ourselves first."

> —Tavis Smiley
> Television & Radio Talk Show Host
> Heard on the Tom Joyner Morning Show, Advocate
> and Author of *How to Make Black America
> Better—Leading African-Americans Speak Out*

"Whether you are saving for a first house, for a col-lege education, or your retirement years, Jesse has a plan for you. This wise and easy-to-follow financial guide will help you live your dreams!"

> —Les Brown, Motivational Speaker and Best Selling
> Author of *It's Not Over Until You Win*

"Jesse Brown's *Pay Yourself First: The African American Guide to Financial Success and Security* is the ultimate survivor's guide! Taking charge of your financial and spiritual wealth today is the best way to ensure a profitable future for you, your family and your community."

> —Terrie M. Williams
> President, The Terrie Williams Agency
> Author of *The Personal Touch: What You Really
> Need to Succeed in Today's Fast-Paced Business
> World*

"Jesse Brown's common sense approach is a surefire way to watch your money grow. For too long we've put our cash in a cookie jar instead of a cookie com-pany. We need a new attitude when it comes to investing. Think about it . . . did you really make any money from your cousin's multi-level marketing program? If you've ever dreamed of, thought about, talked about or put 'save some money' on your things-to-do list, *Pay Yourself First* is a must."

—Myra J., The Tom Joyner Morning Show

"Do not be afraid to plan for a financially secure future for yourself and your family. You can do it, and you should do it today. That's the essence of the sound advice in Jesse Brown's *Pay Yourself First: The African American Guide to Financial Success and Security.*"

—Congressman Jesse L. Jackson, Jr.

"Wall Street brokers may prospect for customers at country clubs, but Mr. Brown's turf is churches, employee cafeterias, and small businesses. Preaching a basic long-term credo—take a bit from each paycheck, put it in the market and wait."

—The *Wall Street Journal*

"Jesse puts into print the same message he delivers to his clients: "Educate yourself, get a plan, and take charge of your financial life. He assures you that the required skills aren't difficult to master, nor is the task as daunting as you fear. For fiscally challenged individuals, Jesse Brown inspires hope. *Pay Yourself First: The African American Guide to Financial Success and Security* can help you create a plan, select the appropriate investments, and stay on track, which, in the final analysis, can leave you in full control."

—William N. Shiebler
Former mutual fund president

More Praise for Jesse Brown,
Author of Invest in the Dream

"Investing in the Dream is a significant resource for African Americans nationwide. I believe it to be a sound beginner's manual for anyone starting out in the investment arena or a fine addition to any investment library. The money is out there; this book can show us all how to make it!"

—Kweisi Mfume, President and CEO, NAACP

"Jesse Brown has provided a tremendous service. Thanks to *Investing in the Dream,* wealth is now within the reach of all who truly desire financial freedom. I have used the same wealth-building strategies, and these too work. Don't just read this book—apply it!"

—Dennis Kimbro, Best-selling Author of "Think and Grow Rich: A Black Choice"

"In a language and style that is easy to grasp with examples that strongly resonate, Jesse Brown will guide you to a clear understanding and better management of your financial future."

—Yolanda King, daughter of the late Martin Luther King, Jr.

"Jesse Brown has created a step-by-step process to help people at all economic levels take charge of their financial future. Complete with clear-cut examples, this book can encourage anyone to overcome fear of the stock market and begin a life of financial security."

—Stedman Graham, Best-selling author of *You Can Make It Happen*

PAY YOURSELF FIRST

*The African American Guide to
Financial Success and Security*

JESSE B. BROWN

Your easy steps to
MAKING and SAVING
MORE MONEY

An Amber Book

John Wiley & Sons, Inc.
New York • Chichester • Weinheim • Brisbane • Toronto • Singapore

Published by John Wiley & Sons, Inc.
Published simultaneously in Canada.

Produced by Amber Books Publishing
    1334 East Chandler Blvd.
    Suite 5-D67
    Phoenix, AZ 85048
        Tony Rose, Publisher and Editorial Director
        Sam Peabody, Associate Publisher
        Yvonne Rose, Senior Editor

This publication is designed to provide accurate and authoritative information in regard
to the subject matter covered. It is sold with the understanding that the publisher is not
engaged in rendering professional services. If professional advice or other expert assistance is required, the services of a competent professional person should be sought.

ISBN 0-471-15897-6

Printed in the United States of America

10 9 8 7 6 5 4 3 2 1

To my wife, Delores, who inspires,
and my daughter Khalilah,
who validates all that I do.

Acknowledgments

I'd like to thank especially Carole Hall, Editor in Chief, Wiley Black Interest Books; Tony Rose, Publisher & CEO, Amber Books Publishing; Yvonne Rose, Senior Editor, Amber Books Publishing; Jan Miller, my literary agent; and special thanks to Darnel Pulphus, graphic designer.

I have not attempted to cite in the text all the authorities and sources consulted in the preparation of this book. The list would include departments of the federal government, libraries, industrial institutions, periodicals, and many individuals. Scores of people have contributed information, illustrations, and inspirations toward the publishing of *Pay Yourself First: The African American Guide to Financial Success and Security.*

Table of Contents

About the Author

Jesse B. Brown is a graduate of the Kellogg School of Management at Northwestern University, Evanston, Illinois, where he was named Alumnus of the Year. He is also immediate past president of the National Association of Securities Professionals—Chicago Chapter and has earned Investment Advisor of the Year honors from one of the largest mutual fund companies in America.

Before joining the financial service industry, Brown served as a Special Assistant to the President of the Joint Center for Political Studies in Washington, DC, and as Deputy to the Assistant Secretary of the Treasury under President Jimmy Carter. He later joined Kidder Peabody as a stockbroker specializing in municipal markets.

Jesse B. Brown is known as one of the country's most renowned financial planners. He is president/CEO, majority stockholder, and Midwest managing director of Krystal Investment Management, Inc., which oversees millions of dollars in mutual funds, stocks, and bonds for his investor clients. According to Brown:"As African Americans, we must realize the significance of paying ourselves first and investing in ourselves, our families, our children, our schools, our churches, our businesses and our communities. We must see ourselves realistically in our society and project what we want to be and put the plan in order. Then, we, as a burgeoning and vibrant independent people, will begin to see most of our goals and commitments realized."

Jesse B. Brown has written *Pay Yourself First: The African American Guide to Financial Success and Security* as the first step in your journey toward financial independence. His first title, *Investing in the Dream,* is a past best-seller on *Essence* magazine's Black Board Best Seller's List for hardcover nonfiction books and was selected as the 2001 Chicago Black Book Fair's Book of the Year.

Foreword

Economic opportunity is, as we lawyers say, the pathway to power. Any society that's truly "of the people, for the people and by the people" must share its economic bounty with all the people. While black folk must help shape the debate over the rules of the game, we must also resolve to play the game hard, whether we like the rules, or not.

Fifty years ago Jackie Robinson seized greatness. He didn't wait for permission to be great. We have an unprecedented talent pool to take our people to an entirely new plateau of economic power. Thanks to their own ability and thanks, yes, to affirmative action, which opened the doors for brilliant young people, we now have a twenty-year supply of awesomely talented MBAs, attorneys and undergraduate business and marketing majors who have the requisite skills and mindset. We have scores of management consultants, plant managers, product managers, salespeople and even a smattering of senior executives who've worked inside corporations in the core business.

Jesse Brown, author of *Pay Yourself First: The African American Guide to Financial Success and Security* is part of this whole new generation of African American entrepreneurs who are doing marvelous things, not just in minority markets, but in mainstream markets as well.

This is the next civil rights frontier. The key question is: Are we players? Shame on us if we let this opportunity slip by, only to moan years from now that we're still on the outside looking in.

Economic power provides the fuel for exercising political clout. For mobilizing our ballot power so that politicians who covet our vote don't take us for granted. For influencing national election outcomes, as we've learned the hard way of late, shapes the composition of those federal courts that ultimately rule on issues close to home, like affirmative action and contract set-asides. Economic power generates the wealth.

—Hugh B. Price, President,
National Urban League

Introduction

ESTABLISH YOUR FOUNDATION

"When you are dependent, you lack control. When you are independent, you gain control."

—JESSE B. BROWN
Krystal Investment Management

There are two choices to make when it comes to establishing your financial security. You can do absolutely nothing at all and let your financial security be at the mercy of whatever circumstances arise. Or you can start to learn about money and begin to build your financial security. Most people who do nothing end up with nothing but more struggles and empty pockets. The fact that you are reading this book tells me you want to empower yourself with knowledge and information and are ready to do whatever is necessary to establish your and your family's financial success and security. Together, as African Americans looking for financial security for our children, our families, and ourselves, we will take one step at a time. I assure you, the outcome will be a great sense of pride, accomplishment, a new sense of peace and financial security.

Establishing financial security is not an easy task. Unfortunately, a lot of us find this new world complex and confusing, but it can be done. For most of us getting started, the pain of thinking and acting differently, can be a most difficult challenge. It means you have to consciously set aside a little time, make a plan, change some of your spending and savings habits, and then stick to the plan. In other words, you must be willing to commit yourself to success. You're already ahead because you've taken the first step by reading this book!

This book is about taking control and creating solutions. I am going to give you the information, steps, and principles you need to undo debt, make sound financial decisions and investments, and create a world where you are in control, building toward your and your family's financial wealth and security. The choice you have made by reading this book will lead you toward your goals and away from the quicksand of frustration and fear, where so many of us find ourselves. This book will help you create the foundation for your own unique personal goals and commitments, and make them a reality. ***By reading a chapter a day, you will increase your knowledge and information, thus preparing you for a successful financial future.*** (*These are your steps to success. Read a chapter a day, carefully, and you will begin to build a successful financial future for you, your children, and your family.)

Let's get started, and remember the goal—money, money, money—how to get it and how to keep it.

—Jesse B. Brown

Chapter 1

RULES OF THE FINANCIAL ROAD

"The future is purchased by the present."

—DAISY LEE BATES
Journalist

Money. There are songs about it, everyone wants it, people spend their lives trying to make more of it or trying to make it faster. People say love makes the world go round, but to a great degree it is money that does that, because without it we can't have the necessities of life—food, clothing, shelter. And if we don't have the necessities, we certainly can't consider acquiring the luxuries!

Despite this, most people don't know the rules of the financial road. The fact is that money is both a cause and an effect. It's a solution to most problems, if you have it. If you don't have it, a problem is created.

COULD YOU BE A MILLIONAIRE?

Most African Americans may wish they were millionaires but can't imagine ever being one. You probably can't think past your next paycheck and what needs that money must satisfy. Believe it or not, just by reading this book you could be well on your way to becoming that millionaire.

The truth is most of us do earn a fortune in our lifetime—for instance, the average person may work from age twenty to age sixty-five. That's 45 years' worth of opportunity. Let's assume you will average about $30,000 over your working lifetime. That's $1.35 million. Now, consider if you earn more than this amount. I hope you see where I'm going with this example. Regardless of how modest your income, chances are great that a fortune will pass through your hands within your lifetime, and if you combine whatever your spouse makes, you come even closer to being that millionaire than you may have thought.

You might be asking yourself, "Why, then, are so many African Americans retiring in poverty?" The answer lies in one basic fact— a lot of us have never learned how to make our money work for us.

IT'S WHAT YOU KEEP THAT COUNTS

We know having income is important, but what you keep is what counts the most. This might be a good time to go back and figure what your average income will be over your working life. Multiply that by the number of years you've worked so far. Now ask yourself, "How much of that figure have I saved?" Shocking, isn't it?

What happens to those people just like you who live from paycheck to paycheck? The demands on their money are intense because they are pulled in hundreds of different directions, all at the same time. Most people sit down each month and write the same categories of what needs to be paid: mortgage or rent payments, car payments and maintenance, school expenses, food, utilities, personal hygiene. The list seems endless. When you are finished satisfying this list of necessities, however, there's not a lot left.

Who can save for the future when it's hard enough just living day by day? You can, as long as you don't make the five major mistakes than can keep you in financial distress. They are:

1. Lack of understanding about how money works
2. Lack of financial goals
3. Lack of a financial plan
4. Overpaying for the most basic items
5. Waiting and doing nothing

If you can claim one or more of these mistakes as your own, don't worry. You have company, because most African Americans can make the same claim. You've heard misery loves company. If you learn how to overcome these common mistakes, you will leave them and the misery behind, and move toward a much brighter future.

WHY THE AVERAGE AFRICAN AMERICAN FAILS TO PLAN FOR THE FUTURE

Believing it's possible for you to change your financial situation is the most important challenge you face. There are many reasons why the average African American fails to plan for the future. Let's look at three common fallacies.

1. There isn't enough money to manage. Since we don't have any money left after taking care of our household, why do

we need to learn how to manage our money? There are always ways to free up money, no matter how tight it is!

2. I don't have the time. Everyone is so busy. I am no exception. So it stands to reason, I don't have the time. Right? Wrong! You can't afford not to learn.

3. I don't have the knowledge. If you go to any bookstore or library, you will find shelves and shelves of books by people who have plenty of advice to give on managing money. Those who are rich know only one thing you don't—knowledge is available equally to everyone. It just requires a little effort, and if you borrow from your library, it won't cost anything but time.

The Foundation Can Be Built

The right foundation of a home ensures it will be strong, withstanding the most powerful attacks from the elements. Your financial foundation is no different. A clear goal and a definite plan are the cement and mortar of your finances. Just set a goal that everyone in your family agrees on, and work toward it together by following your plan. Nothing forces you to think abut what is really important than setting a goal. It can cause you to reflect and make choices differently from what you have done in the past.

Some years ago, a man named Napoleon Hill developed a simple formula for becoming financially independent. His formula is still as solid today as it was when he wrote his book in 1937! His six steps to reaching your goals are:

1. You must have a specific goal.
2. You must have a specific time to achieve your goal.
3. You must write down your goal.
4. You must develop a plan to achieve your goal.
5. You must decide what price you are willing to pay.
6. You must think about your goal every day.

Condensed from *Think and Grow Rich* by Napoleon Hill, originally published in 1937.

You have to know where you're going in order to get there. What do you want your life to be like? What do you want to happen? How can you reach your goal? If you set a goal, four things will happen: (1) You will have an incentive to make the necessary sacrifices; (2) You will be able to see your progress because you will record it every step of the way; (3) You won't lose track of your successes; and (4) you will be able to celebrate milestones.

Of course, you will want both short- and long-term goals. Short-term goals are specific and can be realized in a short span of time. They also require a short period of discipline and enable you to see the results of your efforts. Vacations, a new bike, or replacing a summer wardrobe are examples of short-term goals.

Long-term goals are for major purchases or large cash accumulations. They require more planning, discipline, and patience over a longer period of time. Building a home, sending your children to college, planning for retirement, or accumulating $50,000 in your savings account are some common examples of long-term goals.

After you know your destination, you need a map to guide the way. Financially speaking, your map is your plan. Sometimes, because of unforeseen circumstances, your plan must be modified. These circumstances can be changes in your personal life or changes in the economy. With a little effort and planning, however, you can develop a plan that will make a difference in your family's future.

IT'S TIME TO GET SERIOUS

Many people believe that budgeting requires sacrifice and effort. But it doesn't have to be that way. As long as you keep it simple, you can master this concept. Begin with the same categories that you use to determine where your paycheck goes (Remember, your mortgage or rent payments, car payments and maintenance, school expenses, food, utilities, and personal hygiene).

Your checkbook can be a good place to start. You'll be able to determine where money is going because bills and automatic cash station (ATM) withdrawals are registered there. For a month or so, monitor your expenses while you make an effort not to overspend or waste money. You'll be able to quickly determine what you are spending, what's out of line, and where you can save.

When the average person uses this approach, they're shocked to see how much money disappears in a week's time. Sometimes you withdraw money and, if you keep no record, you find yourself wondering how and where it was spent.

Controlling what you spend is how you take control of your money. It gives you an opportunity to rearrange your spending habits and find ways to save. What's the end result?

The more often you use this simple process, the better you will be able to live within a budget by constantly deciding what to spend and how to adjust your budget. It will soon become second nature, and you'll be helping yourself in spite of those spending urges that flare up from time to time.

CONSTANTLY REFLECT ON WHAT'S IMPORTANT

However, as a people, we seem to encounter an endless array of distractions. More often than not, we are forced to spend our money on emergencies or necessities; and when we finally do have something to go shopping with, we may buy what we want rather than what we need. Keeping your priorities straight helps you resist the urge to buy on impulse. Whether you shop for groceries, computer equipment, or clothing, you'll notice impulse items conveniently shelved near the cash register. One of the strategies of marketing is understanding how impulse buying can make the most frugal person buy an item not on their list.

The key to successful money management is to distinguish a need from a want. You can have anything your money can buy, but do you need everything you purchase? Questioning yourself by distinguishing between a "need" and a "want" is a good tool that will keep you from leaving your cash in the store and help you to leave it in your wallet.

Most of us know someone who always seems to have cash readily available, only to be in a bind when times suddenly get hard. These people focus on their "wants" while ignoring their needs for savings and a healthy financial outlook.

A DREAM TURNS INTO A NIGHTMARE

Starting your financial plan is a dream, whereas procrastinating is a nightmare. Don't try to do everything at once. Be patient with yourself. Just start moving in the right direction, pacing yourself to go the distance, and don't get discouraged. Eventually, you'll see progress.

Did You Get the Message?

Since you've gotten this far, you've already learned several important things about financial security. Take this quiz and test your knowledge. Answer True or False to each statement.

1. Building a home is an example of a long-term goal.

2. Sending your children to college is an example of a short-term goal.

3. Lack of understanding about how money works is a major financial-planning mistake.

4. Overpaying for the most basic items is a major financial-planning mistake.

5. Waiting and doing nothing is a major financial-planning mistake.

6. Most people earn a fortune in their lifetime.

7. Having a specific time frame in which to achieve your goal helps in building a financial foundation.

8. There are always ways to free up money no matter how tight it is.

9. If you set goals, you will have an incentive to make the necessary sacrifices.

10. Controlling what you spend gives you an opportunity to find ways to save.

Key

1. T	6. T
2. F	7. T
3. T	8. T
4. T	9. T
5. T	10. T

Chapter 2

YOUR FOUR BASIC BUILDING BLOCKS

"Most people search high and wide for the keys to success. If they only knew the key to their dreams lies within."
—GEORGE WASHINGTON CARVER
Scientist

The foundation of financial success is built on four basic points that can help you control your money. Being in control makes your money work for you, not against you. There are many "fine points" of money management, but these basic guidelines will, by themselves, lead you to the path of financial success.

I believe that most African Americans, like you and me, intend to make our families financially secure. Unfortunately, many of us haven't taken the simple, basic steps to build financial security. In order to build financial security, you must first take a good look at where your money currently goes, then decide on some very specific goals. Once you have these answers firmly in your mind, you are ready to develop a plan by implementing the following four basic building blocks toward success. Let's take a close look at them.

BUILDING BLOCK #1: ALWAYS PAY YOURSELF FIRST

When you think about it, every goal you've ever reached first started with you—your thoughts, your dreams, your desires. The first step to becoming financially secure is no different. You must literally put yourself first before everyone else. That's right. For once in your life, it's going to be something positive to be selfish! Paying yourself first will reap rewards for your entire family. This means before you pay your rent or your utilities, or consider any other demands on your money, put your family's future first.

When you consider all the facts, it makes good sense and it's the only way to reach your goals. So before you acknowledge anyone else's claim on your money, always pay yourself. What's the easiest way to do this? By consistently saving or investing the same amount from your primary source of income—your paycheck.

A basic rule of thumb is to save a minimum 10 percent of your income. Each time your income increases, remember to adjust this amount up to 10 percent of that new amount. If you can save more than the 10 percent minimum, that's great! This simple investment will start you moving in the right direction.

The Two Basic Savings Accounts You Should Consider for Emergencies and Investments

A complete savings program has two types of basic accounts: one for emergency funds and another for long-term funds.

We always seem to get more than our fair share of unforeseen emergencies or unexpected expenses, such as the loss of a job, a serious and costly medical problem, car problems, or major household repairs. Events such as these usually happen suddenly and without warning. So, it's wise to establish an emergency account first before you consider any type of long-range savings plan.

With this emergency fund firmly established, you are protected against having your finances destroyed or being forced to withdraw from your second long-range savings account. A good rule of thumb is to have three months' salary in this emergency fund.

Helpful Points About Your Savings Accounts

Point One: Harness the desire to use your emergency account as a checking account. Once you've deposited your planned amount, don't use it unless it's a real emergency. Make vacations, fun activities, or luxury purchases part of your budgeting process, funded only through disposable income left after the savings have been set aside.

Point Two: Make sure your emergency fund is easily accessible to you. Savings or investment plans that pay the best rates of return most often have enormous withdrawal penalties. This means they won't work well for this type of fund. On the other hand, money-market funds may be better suited because they offer a rate of return that's fairly competitive. They also allow easy access to your money and in cases of emergency, you may even have check-writing privileges.

Point Three: Your long-term savings or investment fund represents money saved toward retirement, a new home, college, and other long-range goals.

This fund does not have to be readily accessible, although it's still wise to avoid opportunities for heavy withdrawal penalties whenever possible. There are a wide range of vehicles available for long-term savings.

Today's Simplest Savings Vehicle: Direct Deposit

The concept of direct deposit was created in 1976 as a way for individuals to conveniently receive Social Security checks. Since then, it has become the most popular way to provide for both short-term savings and long-term investments.

Let's face it, when money is in your pocket or checkbook, the ability to remember what the money is allotted for is sometimes very difficult and the temptation to spend it is irresistible. Therefore, when you receive funds after the direct deposit is fulfilled, your savings or investment is ensured up front.

The beauty of this is that you don't have to rely on your discipline. You can arrange for your employer to set aside a certain amount from your payroll each month and direct the deposit into the fund of your choice.

At this point, you probably have a better understanding of the basic concept of paying yourself first and why it is one of the strongest building blocks toward creating your financial foundation.

BUILDING BLOCK #2: TIME IS POWER

It's said that the only two things life gives you are opportunity and time. You may not be able to control opportunity, but more often than not, you can control time. This is because time is one of life's most precious gifts, "given" almost equally to everyone. Except for unexpected tragedies, with today's technology, most people will live long lives. This means that in your lifetime there's still ample opportunity to work financial miracles.

Time is probably the most underrated commodity when creating a financial plan. Yet, in building a firm financial foundation, it is without a doubt the most important tool that we, as African Americans, have. The correct use of time can overcome issues that might be considered shortcomings: modest income, modest rates of return, even poor habits. However, with time, what was previously considered a disastrous financial situation can be righted. Combined with an adequate rate of return and consistency, time is a powerful tool for achieving the financial security that we all desire.

Consider this simple example: Suppose the day you were born, your parents deposited $1,000 in an account. Let's further assume it was invested for a modest 6 percent rate of return. If that investment was untouched until you turned age sixty-five, that initial $1,000 would have become $44,000—without your ever having added another penny!

Unfortunately, most people don't have parents with such financial foresight or ability. Just remember, no matter when someone starts saving, time can still work to their advantage.

Assuming you can't find money to save is the biggest financial mistake most people make. The truth of the matter is that almost everyone with an income can find something to save. It doesn't have to be a dramatic amount of money, which is good news. But it does require desire and discipline.

Let's say, beginning at age twenty-five until retirement, you could save a mere $5 a week. Could you find a way to save even more? The more you can manage to comfortably save, the more effectively time can work in your favor. This is a significant factor that holds great influence over the growth of your dollar amount.

The Penalty or Price of Waiting

Knowing how to make time work to your advantage is crucial. It can't be overemphasized. There are two choices available if you want to accumulate the money necessary to reach your goals. They involve time and growth.

You can make time the most important component of your plan, or you can waste time by assuming money is the most important component. The average person doesn't have a lot of money. But, when viewed in this light, it should be realized that time is the most critical factor in your financial success.

While you're young, you or your parents can save small amounts and end up with thousands of dollars merely by taking advantage of time. The alternative is waiting until you're older to begin saving. You can take this route, but it means you must save much more in a shorter period of time.

Consider the example of the parents who deposited money when their child was born. What if they had waited until the child was sixteen years old to start? Moreover, what if they had waited until their child was 40?

You have the power to make time your best friend or your worst enemy. You can make it your friend by starting to save right now—today, if possible. If you have children, remember the example of the wise parents. Small amounts of money set aside when your child is born can make a tremendous difference twenty years down the road.

Combine Consistency with Time

You can now understand how time and growth can be the best of friends. It's a hard fact, but not all African Americans have $1,000 to deposit all at once. So, if this is your situation, it's a good idea to save small amounts at specific intervals in order to build wealth. Always remember, consistency can be the fuel that boosts your desired investment and makes it skyrocket.

Building Block #3: The Advantage of Compounding

Let's return again to the example of the parents who deposited $1,000 at 6 percent interest in an account when their child was born. The annual interest would be $60, based on that 6 percent rate. If we multiplied that rate by sixty-five years, the $60 would have grown to $3,900. How could their child have over $44,000 to withdraw at age sixty-five? This is the advantage and power of compound interest—one of the most important keys to attaining wealth. Here's how compounding works.

During the first year of the initial deposit, if the 6 percent or $60 was added to the $1,000, the investment would change to $1,060. During the second year, the 6 percent rate of interest would then be calculated on the new balance of $1,060. This would bring the interest credited to $63.60, making the total balance $1,123. Each year, as the account grew, the interest rate would be calculated on the new account total, including all interest payments.

Based on compound interest, the $1,000 would grow to $44,000! With the power and advantage of compound interest working for you, you now understand how quickly an initial saving of a few hundred dollars can become a thousand.

BUILDING BLOCK #4: ANOTHER IMPORTANT FACTOR: RATE OF RETURN

The rate of return is another critical key often overlooked when building financial security. Rate of return and interest rate are interchangeable terms. The impact of the rate of return combined with time may initially seem minor. However, when considering the difference of a few percentage points over time, the impact is significant.

It can be difficult to realize what a dramatic effect a higher rate of return can have. You'd logically think if you earned a 10 percent rate of return instead of 5 percent, your money would merely double. This isn't so. Once again, taking into account the power of compound interest, that 5 percent difference, added up over time, can add thousands of dollars to any investment made for you and your family.

Let's go back once more to the example of the parents who deposited the initial $1,000 for their child at a rate of 6 percent. What could the child have withdrawn at age sixty-five if the account had earned a higher rate of return? If we consider the difference between a 6 percent and a 9 percent rate of return, the parents would have built $226,000 in financial security. At 12 percent, you can see the difference would be over a million dollars!

Since your main objective in saving is to accumulate as much cash as possible, understanding the rate of return you receive on your savings or investment account is crucial.

There are two ways to reach this objective: Save more money and accept a lower rate of return, or save less and receive a higher rate of return. Not many of us can save more, but we can all do a little research and concentrate on getting a higher rate. In other words, make our money really work for us.

KEEP YOUR EYES FOCUSED ON THE FUTURE
The Formula for Success

When we combine the three essentials we just discussed, we have a formula that guarantees financial success and is easily understood:

$$Time + Consistency + Rate\ of\ Return = Maximum\ Growth$$

The Pitfalls of Status

A lot of intelligent and educated African Americans are currently living on substandard retirement incomes. They might have gotten caught up in the "status trap." In order to "keep up with the Joneses"—to have the nicest house, the most luxurious car, the most elaborate or exotic vacation—they could be shortchanging their futures.

Consider what can do the most for your future security: a fancy luxury car, with its big debt and high monthly payment, or $30,000.

The Choice Is Yours

If you choose savings or investments of $30,000, you'd have no debt and over $67,000 in your long-term savings at the end of twenty years. If you choose status and purchase a luxury car, you've relied on something transient that will last a much shorter time, and which, in the long run, will have to be replaced.

Did You Get the Message?

You are already making progress, just by reading this book. Take this quiz and confirm how much you've learned so far. Answer true or false to each statement.

1. In order to build financial security, you must first take a good look at where your money currently goes, then decide on some specific goal.

2. Always paying yourself first is a building block toward financial success.

3. Time + Consistency + Rate of Return = Maximum Growth.

4. Getting caught in the status trap can shortchange your future.

5. It is best to set up an emergency fund before establishing a long-term savings plan.

6. Assuming you can't find money to save is the biggest financial mistake people make.

7. Time is the most underrated commodity when creating a financial plan.

8. Saving more money and accepting a low rate of return will help you accumulate more cash.

9. Compounded interest can help your investments grow.

10. People overemphasize the important role time plays in investing.

Key

1. T	6. T
2. T	7. T
3. T	8. T
4. T	9. T
5. T	10. F

Chapter 3

BEAT TODAY'S FINANCIAL CANCER: DEBT

"Worry is interest paid on trouble before it is due."

—MIRIAM MAKEBA
Folk Singer

The biggest threat to your financial success is debt. Everyone has some type of debt—African Americans seem to have more. "Buying on time" unfortunately, has become a way of life for too many of us. It has become a fact of life since Isaac Singer invented the idea in 1856.

Were he alive today, he'd be astonished at the impact of his simple idea. Let me explain. Mr. Singer wanted to find a way to sell his sewing machines, which cost $125. This was a time when most families were struggling financially. So he came up with a simple plan. He had the families give him $5, take the machine home, and pay $5 per month until the debt was completely settled. Not only did his plan spark sales, he unknowingly invented a new way to purchase goods.

With that success in mind, in 1916 Arthur Morris pioneered the installment loan. When we look around at what's available for consumers to purchase, it's hard to imagine functioning in today's economy without credit.

WHY IS DEBT A THREAT?

For many African Americans, "impulse shopping" is an over-buying syndrome that can lead to a variety of problems in the future. None of us set out to "get in debt." We simply expect to satisfy all our needs immediately. The problem is, most often what we term a "need" is actually a "want or desire." This "instant gratification" has enabled us to purchase items now and worry about how to pay for them later.

HOW COULD SOMETHING SO INNOVATIVE BECOME SO TREACHEROUS?

You may have good intentions to pace your credit buying with your income, but suddenly it's out of balance. It happens before you know it. Your parents may not have had the luxury of owning credit cards, and therefore you didn't grow up understanding that they might cause you to "ruin your credit." Unfortunately, there are thousands of African Americans who find themselves in this predicament. See if this scenario sounds familiar:

- With your first credit card in hand, you charge a few items and pay off the balance each month. Then you realize how great this is for big-ticket items that you can't pay off so easily.
- Perhaps because of this big item, or many small items, your balance begins to gradually increase, becoming more than you can pay off each month. So now you resort to paying the minimum required balance.
- You notice that the interest charges and fees eat up a huge part of your payment, rather than whittling down the principal. The principal builds at a faster rate.
- Unexpectedly an emergency happens, and you don't have cash to pay for it, so you charge it, promising yourself you will pay it off when the bill comes.
- Now the principal balance is even larger, and it takes all your disposable income to pay the minimum.
- Your bank raises your credit limit, and you breathe a little easier.
- Another emergency happens, and since your credit limit is higher, you put the charge on your credit card.
- Something happens and you reach your new limit. A preapproved credit-card application arrives unsolicited in the mail. So you apply for it and get another card.
- The disposable income you once had is almost gone. You decide to take a trip out of town, so you get a cash advance, which is also charged to your credit card.
- As your balance grows, the interest on your charges takes up more and more of your monthly payment. Now the principal seems almost at a standstill.
- You've now used your charge accounts to their maximum. You don't remember how this happened because you have

little to show for the charges. After you satisfy the other bills, your disposal income won't even pay the minimum due. You start incurring hefty late fees.

Thousands of people are in this predicament. If you were able to recognize yourself at any point in this scenario, you need to get control of your debt. Were you able to point out some common credit mistakes that worked against you? If not, here are some common credit mistakes you may be making:

1. Not placing enough value on your credit. Good credit is really valuable in today's economy. On the other hand, bad credit creates a negative financial profile that works against you and is available for all to see. A lot of African Americans get caught with a negative credit history, which threatens the American Dream of purchasing a home. Unfortunately, bad credit can cause your so-called creditor to reject your application based on your record of abuse.

2. Desire for status overruling your common sense. Many companies advertise that their prestigious gold or platinum credit cards are for people who desire and deserve the best. By nature, a lot of people like to flaunt these "status symbols." Just the image of who fits that profile makes you want to be one of the "haves" because it means a higher credit limit and more frills. It probably means higher annual fees also. Try to avoid paying for status.

3. Be satisfied with your credit limit. When you receive your credit card, you are assigned a limit, which means increased temptation to spend. Just because it's offered, you don't have to accept the new limit. Practice common sense and harness your ego to accept what isn't necessary.

4. Asking for the maximum duration of a loan to get lower payments. It's hard enough for us to get a loan, and when we do, many times we want to stretch out the life of a loan in order to get lower monthly payments. Loan companies love this scenario because they receive more interest payments over

the life of the loan. Consider selecting the shortest payment period possible. You may also have to consider if the purchase is really necessary, particularly if the life of the loan is very extensive.

5. Being unaware of your interest rate and fees. Fees vary. Don't fall into the trap of accepting "easy money." Before you apply for or accept a credit card, make sure you know its interest rate and annual fee. You may be able to find a lower rate just by doing some investigating. It's true, for many of us, that the convenience of a credit card is by far more important than the cost of what you buy, especially with the status it brings, but the problem is the rates and fees that you are charged to use the card.

   Some cards charge a once-a-year fee for the privilege of using their card. Other cards have differing rates, depending on the type of card. In order to know exactly what your interest rate will be, it's a good idea to read the "fine print" on the back of the monthly statement or the introductory letter before you decide to apply for a new card.

Now that we've discussed some common mistakes, let's discuss some simple remedies:

1. Cut those cards in half or throw them out. This is an easy way to stop using those cards.
2. Keep the balances low and pay them off. Make a habit of paying off balances. Always remember that paying $100 on 19 percent is a greater savings than the same amount deposited in your investment
3. If your debt is at a crisis level, investigate a consolidation loan. These loans are especially for people who are making efforts to get a hold on their finances. You allow a financial institution to pay off all your creditors. They, in turn, combine all the balance amounts into one loan with one monthly payment. This will help you get your finances in order and your creditors will be paid. It's a win-win situation.

4. A consolidation loan is an opportunity to learn discipline. This loan gives you an opportunity to learn how to use credit wisely. More important, it could even help you understand that paying cash for the majority of your purchases is a great option.

Managing debt is one of the most important pillars of positive financial health. If you don't learn how to manage your debt, you will never find the security you desire because of the cash drain it creates.

You will begin to understand how debt robs you of the ability to maintain the emergency fund that is so crucial to your stability in times of financial uncertainty. The bottom line? Develop discipline by using your credit cards only for emergencies. If you have an impulse to buy, make sure you are reaching for cash, not plastic.

MORE ON INTEREST: SAVINGS ADVANTAGE, CHARGING DISADVANTAGE

In an earlier discussion, we talked about compound interest and what a positive difference it makes when you are trying to accumulate funds. There is, however, a negative side to compounding. It occurs when you pay only the minimum balance on your credit cards. In cases such as these, interest charges are added to the principal each month. When you get your new monthly statement, the balance is a combination of the principal plus the interest charged for the use of that company's money, and that amount gets compounded again.

As this cycle continues, you start to see your money actually working against you. Now you understand how something you buy on credit today can still be on your credit card years after it's been purchased. In some cases, the item has been discarded, yet the charge is still alive and well.

Does this mean you should avoid having credit cards? Not at all. Many stores require a driver's license and a credit card before they will accept your check. Most rental-car companies and hotels won't even make reservations unless you use a credit card as a guarantee. Some restaurants even refuse to take cash!

This means it's a good idea to have one credit card for the situations I mentioned.

Today's Most Common Loan: The Home Mortgage

Whether renting or buying, housing is our most important expense. If you are considering owning a home—and all African Americans should try—it is most likely the one long-term debt that is unavoidable. It's the most significant debt you'll ever have. At least 29 percent of our disposable income is spent on housing.

So saving money on your mortgage can make a great difference in your financial picture. Let's look at some ways to save on your mortgage.

Increase Your Savings

One of the best ways to save on your mortgage is to make additional payments on the principal each month. This will allow you to pay off the debt early.

Some banks and savings and loans offer these types of mortgage-acceleration programs that can help you reduce the "real cost" of owning a home.

Let's say you borrowed $100,000 for a home at 9 percent for 30 years. Your monthly payments would be $804.62 per month in principal and interest.

Yet, over the thirty years, you will actually pay $289,663, of which $189,663 will be interest. You could "prepay" your loan and reduce its life to twenty-five years simply by paying $34.58 more in principal each month. This means you could reduce your total interest by $37,903 and pay the mortgage off five years ahead of schedule. This is another example how a small amount can make a big difference if it is consistently applied.

An unconventional method we hear little about is to pay your loan in two-week increments. This will reduce the amount of interest that adds up on the unpaid balance over a month's time. In addition, you'll be able to pay off your loan in little more than half the time.

Don't Forget the Significance of Rate

The same benefits one percentage point can make in your savings or investment accounts also applies to your mortgage. Using the same scenario we discussed above, you could save $25,509 in interest over the period of the loan by paying 8 percent interest rather than 9 percent. Isn't this reason enough to seek out the best rate available?

Did You Get the Message?

We often pay our bills first and then spend whatever is left as soon as we get it. But there's a better way. In order to build financial security we must first take a good look at where our money currently goes, decide on a specific goal, and stick to it. Look at the following scenarios to see how you score. Answer True or False to each statement.

1. The biggest threat to your financial security is debt.
2. Credit card interest charges and fees keep you out of debt.
3. Good credit is really valuable in today's economy.
4. Always push your credit limit to the max.
5. Being aware of your interest rate and fees helps you to minimize debt.
6. Impulse shopping is an overbuying syndrome that can lead to a variety of problems in the future.
7. Ignoring your interest rate and fees is a debt remedy.
8. Keeping your balances low and paying them off is a debt remedy.

9. Cutting up your credit cards and tossing them is a debt remedy.

10. One of the best ways to save on your mortgage is to make additional payments on the principal each month.

Key:

1. T	6. T
2. F	7. F
3. T	8. T
4. F	9. T
5. T	10. T

Chapter 4

YOU CAN TAKE CONTROL— BE STRONG!

"It doesn't matter what you're trying to accomplish. It's all a matter of discipline ... I was determined to discover what life held beyond the inner city streets."

—WILMA RUDOLPH
Olympic Champion

here's no secret to why a lot of African Americans have trouble moving toward financial security. We all struggle with the same issue: How can we build security when everything around us seems so insecure? The answer lies first in deciding to take control and move toward building financial security one brick at a time. This means there are a number of decisions to make about your money and your habits, both positive and negative. Actually, the decisions you make on a daily basis have a profound effect on your financial foundation.

There is only one major factor in solving our financial challenges—it's not the government, the institutions around us, the politicians, or our neighbors. We are at the center of our financial security because only we uniquely understand the goals and dreams of our family.

Perhaps this is why you are no further along in solving these problems. Don't dismay, look no further than your mirror. You are the greatest asset and ally your family has!

DEPENDENCE—OUR BIGGEST FINANCIAL MISTAKE

For the most part, we have become accustomed to relying on someone else for our financial decisions. We may have done this because we felt they knew more or perhaps we were just insecure, not wanting to make mistakes. We have relied on banks, savings and loans, mortgage lenders, and other types of financial institutions to help solve our financial problems. Sometimes we blindly accept whatever advice they offer.

Don't misunderstand me, advice can be helpful. It can also cost thousands of dollars over your lifetime. When you consider this advice, isn't the end result most often some product that you are sold? Additionally, when you turn your financial future over to someone else, they have decided what products suit the needs of you and your family. Financial independence, however, means independence from too much influence.

In order to feel secure financially, you must give up your dependence and seize control of your life. Stop counting on others to protect your American Dream. What does this really mean? It means you must begin taking an active role in making decisions that are going to determine your family's future. It means that you have to decide you're going to develop some winning habits that will pay off. It means realizing nobody cares more about your dreams than you.

Know What You Can Control

I know it sounds impossible, but you can gain more control over your future. Before you gain this control, you first have to know what you can control.

Most often, the reason that African Americans feel insecure in any area of our lives is because we have opted to give control over our lives to others. Financially speaking, the solution is to learn the basic rules of the game. We can learn how money works and how to use it wisely on our behalf.

TABLE 4.1
Elements of Control and Alternate Remedies

You Can *Not* Control	But You *Can* Control
Social Security	Cash for Retirement
Your Employer	Alternate Sources of Income
Taxes	Ways to Reduce Your Taxes
Inflation	Maximize Your Investment Potential
Rising Costs	Save More
The Risk of a Single Investment	Diversification of Your Investments

You Don't Learn Everything in School

Almost everything—a new car, a washing machine, a computer, a VCR, a stereo system, even a toaster!—comes with an instruction booklet.

How to live, how to raise a child, or how to handle money are only a few examples of things that don't come with instructions. Initially you are on your own regarding some of these most important events of your life.

Once you start making money, you can learn ways to be successful in that endeavor. But what you don't know can hurt you and your family, leading to a life of anxiety and defeat instead of peace of mind and achievement.

A lot of us earn high-school diplomas or GEDs, and many of us receive college degrees or even Ph.D.s. Yet nowhere are we taught the basics of how money works. As a result, we are usually left on our own to develop bad money habits, habits that are reinforced over and over again throughout our lives. We may pass these habits down to our children, and thus the cycle repeats itself. Fortunately, sound money principles and good habits can be learned and can make the difference in today's comfort and tomorrow's security.

It stands to reason, therefore, that before we can solve our money problems, we need to learn the basics of how money works. On average, a lot of us spend very little time on financial planning. Historically, during our lifetime, we devote hours and hours to our jobs and spend more time planning vacations than we do our futures.

So today, let's resolve to understand the basic techniques that are used by financial experts everywhere. These are simple principles that can change your thinking, and as a result, your habits, if you follow through on what you learn. When you start to put these principles into action, you will solve your financial problems one by one.

TRIAD FOR SUCCESS

There are only three critical areas you must understand if you are to achieve financial success. They are (1) protection management, (2) asset management, and (3) debt management. Don't be afraid of the terms. You are already functioning in these areas. They compare to income protection (area 1), assets (area 2), and debt (area 3). How well you take control of these areas will determine whether you can protect your family at a reasonable cost, manage your assets to achieve growth, build cash for retirement, and control your debt. These three concepts will show you how to get maximum value at minimum cost and how to build a financial estate and create lasting security.

TAKING CONTROL—THE BEST CHOICES

I started this book talking about choices and rules. It's important for you to remember that not taking control has its own set of consequences. And if you don't start building now, every major event in your life will be a struggle. Your dream home will remain just a dream. College for all your children will be impossible. If you don't take control, you will be faced with no vacations, no fun, and no peace of mind. Because they didn't take control, too many African Americans have seen their dream of a secure and happy retirement for old age replaced with anxiety and poverty at the very time they can do little about it. It's a fact—you must choose. No one else can do this for you. You can put up with the minor pain of discipline now, or do nothing and consciously choose the pain of regret later.

Undoubtedly, you still have time to act if you want your future to be secure and enjoyable. Don't worry, you will still be able to enjoy your life—making it exciting, inspiring, and pleasurable—if you and your spouse pitch in and work together. Your entire family can learn and grow together. You can even include your children in what will be their first lesson in building their own financial security. Consider where you want to be in five, ten, or even twenty years from today and let that be the motivation for all you do from this day forward.

Did You Get the Message?

We can build security when everything around us seems insecure. As African Americans we have been struggling for years, but now we should have some of the answers. Let's see how what you've learned so far. Answer True or False to each statement.

1. You are the greatest asset in planning your financial future.

2. You can't control Social Security, but you can control how much cash you save for retirement.

3. You can control diversification of your investments and ways to reduce your taxes.

4. There are three critical areas you must understand if you are to achieve financial success: protection management, asset management, and debt management.

5. Personal management, spending control, and taking advice well are the major requirements for achieving financial success.

6. Money principles and good habits are too hard to learn and best left to the financial experts.

7. On average, a lot of us spend very little time on financial planning.

8. Most African Americans are taught the basics of how money works.

9. If you don't start building security now, every major event in your future will be a struggle.

10. Many African Americans have seen their dream of a secure retirement replaced with poverty.

Key

1. T	6. F
2. T	7. T
3. T	8. F
4. T	9. T
5. F	10. T

Chapter 5

THE AMERICAN DREAM: ALIVE AND WELL FOR EVERYONE?

"The will to win, the desire to succeed, the urge to reach your full potential ... these are the keys that will unlock the door to personal excellence."

—EDDIE ROBINSON
Grambling University Football Coach

The American Dream has been an important part of the African American's heritage. How many of us still believe in this dream? Today, this so-called dream is close to extinction. Both economic and public opinion studies have recently concluded that the American Dream is becoming more and more of a myth.

If you were born between 1945 and 1964, you are one of millions of people labeled "Baby Boomers." You are also most likely feeling the burden of being part of a boom that has affected America in every economic area. "Boomers" have created havoc in every arena of life, from education to real estate to governmental programs.

In addition, because there are so many of these "Boomers," as they age their future security is also in question. Commonly held beliefs, systems, and even some institutions that seemed guaranteed in the past are either breaking down or have already gone through tremendous change. What was previously assumed to be a "given" as part of the American Dream is now seriously in doubt or already extinct.

The following categories are what people consider when they think of the American Dream. Compare your ideal with these startling realities.

Prosperity—Will It Continue?

It's predicted by many experts that the next generation will be the first in American history to be worse off financially than their parents. As millions of "Baby Boomers" move into retirement, the strain on government programs, initially affordable, will increase. Economists predict the future living standards of all Americans and the American Dream will be threatened and become unviable. Why? Because the "unfunded promises," such as Social Security and Medicare, could result in increased tax rates and reduced disposable income for essential expenses.

STANDARD OF LIVING—CAN IT BE MAINTAINED?

According to various news articles, a new class of workers is emerging and has been labeled the working poor. Several million African Americans live in homes where paychecks and poverty go hand in hand. A family of four, considered at the poverty level when sustained on $14,279, now accounts for more than 9.4 million working Americans. More than half that number are black.

IS THERE STILL A SECURE MIDDLE CLASS?

The hard-working middle class, once revered as the "backbone of America," seems to be one of the most ignored groups in America. When viewed from another aspect, however, this group of Americans file 58 percent of all tax returns, earn 69 percent of the income, and pay 58 percent of all federal income taxes. The very foundation of American life is being threatened because the average paycheck can no longer keep pace with inflation and fend off financial and economic changes.

RETIREMENT: IS IT STILL POSSIBLE?

A worry-free retirement may be the biggest "myth" of all. No generation before us has even had to consider this question. Our parents were secure in the "fact" that the government would take care of them in their old age. The "Baby Boomers" are faced with the startling reality that no one will take care of them but themselves.

SOCIAL SECURITY: IS IT ALIVE AND WELL?

Studies tell us that most young African Americans don't believe they will ever see a Social Security check. Actually, almost half of them believe they have a better chance of seeing visitors from outer space than receiving Social Security benefits! Only 9 percent of them still believe in Social Security! They aren't alone. Here's what Alan Greenspan, chairman of the Federal Reserve Bank, has said time and again:

The basic premise of our largely pay-as-you-go Social Security system is that future productivity will be sufficient to supply promised retirement benefits for current workers. However, even supposing some acceleration in long-term productivity growth from recent experience, at existing rates of savings and capital investment, this is becoming increasingly dubious.

How many of today's senior citizens would be living below the poverty level today if Social Security didn't exist? It would be 50 percent of our entire senior citizen population. Consider what this means for your future: There are no guarantees Social Security will be available in the future.

Job Security: Reality or Myth?

We currently have the strongest job market since the Great Depression. If you would question the average African American, he or she would quickly tell you that they don't feel secure in their jobs or have a fear of being laid off. These are not foolish fears. According to recent census data from the 2000 national survey, the old saying of "last hired, first fired" is still true. Of the millions of workers in the United States who lost their jobs permanently, there was a disportionate number of African Americans. With recession looming in the dark shadows of this economy, African Americans losing their jobs is at its highest figure since the government began keeping track of displaced workers.

In December 2000, American corporations announced that approximately 450,000 individuals would be laid off. Montgomery Ward, a leading national retailer, closed its doors. The Urban League predicted that African Americans would account for more than half of those in the jobless ranks.

Many African Americans believe that long-term security is becoming harder and harder to achieve. It's no longer an expectation but is viewed as an impossible dream, out of reach of the average person. But why do we "feel" so insecure?

Many of us have lost faith in institutions such as the school system, government, the church, even in the future. Why? With all our progress and development, we have somehow made our world increasingly impersonal. Those institutions we used to trust wholeheartedly have let us down. In the past, we all knew who to go to for help. We knew our banker, real-estate agent, or loan officer by name, and even had developed a relationship with them. Because of mergers and takeovers, companies have changed and these relationships have been replaced over and over again. Many companies are only profit oriented, making hundreds of different products while offering little or no service. We have created a society where everyone expects a quick remedy. We have microwave ovens that can deliver meals in a minute, we have drive-in cleaners. The list is endless. We entice shoppers with advertisements that say their dreams will come true if they buy a particular product.

How many of these promises do companies really deliver? They deliver the same remedies as lotteries and casinos—short-term thrills and superficial gains.

It's also been proven that the quick-fix approach to financial dilemmas rarely works. People want more than that. We as African Americans want honest solutions to our problems. Somewhere in the back of our minds we understand that security is the end result of a proven, workable process.

When you look at business relationships, however, no business seems to have the time or desire to focus on the future—because it is so impermanent. But when you consider financial security, this is exactly where your focus must remain.

If you'd talk with your friends and relatives, everyone would probably agree they want financial security. How many of those same people would agree that it is possible? The good news is that anyone can achieve this security if they're willing to learn some simple and powerful basic principles.

Financial security isn't out of reach, and it's available to anyone the moment you decide what's important. Regardless of who you are, nothing matters more than sound information, discipline, and a strong desire to change.

No one wants to end up in financial straits, but if you're not careful, it can sneak up on you when you least expect it. We certainly don't choose to end up this way. Most of us get there by looking at the whole picture, which can be rather overwhelming, and then deciding it can never change. We defeat ourselves by deciding it can't be done, rather than by making small steps day-to-day. By doing this and making sound choices, anyone can create a lifetime of security.

Did You Get the Message?

The "American Dream" has been an important part of the African American's heritage, but today it is close to extinction. See how well you understand the need for serious financial planning. Answer True or False to each statement.

1. In the next 50 years, you are more likely to see a UFO than a Social Security check.

2. The American Dream is a reality of the past that we could never achieve.

3. The working poor could never save enough money to invest.

4. No one wants to end up in financial straits, but if you're not careful, it can sneak up on you when you least expect it.

5. Financial security isn't out of reach; it's available to anyone the moment you decide what's important to you.

6. It's predicted that the next generation will be the first to be better off financially than their parents.

7. As millions of "Baby Boomers" move into retirement, the strain on government programs, which were initially affordable, will increase.

8. The average paycheck keeps pace with inflation and fends off financial and economic changes.

9. A worry-free retirement may be the biggest "myth" of all.

10. Most African Americans believe that long-term security is becoming easier and easier to achieve.

11. There are no guarantees that Social Security will be available in the future.

Key

1.	T	7.	T
2.	F	8.	F
3.	F	9.	T
4.	T	10.	F
5.	T	11.	T
6.	F		

Chapter 6

MONEY AND THE AFRICAN AMERICAN WOMAN

"Do what you do, using your talents and abilities because it makes you happy. In everything you do, have a purpose, principle or ideal that you hold dear and will not compromise if the price is right."

—IYANLA VANZANT

My recollection of growing up in San Antonio, Texas, includes my mother's weekly trips to the Alamo Savings and Loan Office as she deposited receipts for her Eastern Star Lodge. As she deposited those receipts, she would show me how to fill out a deposit slip so that I too could make a bank deposit. As treasurer for her organization, she was putting money to work for her lodge as I put money to work for my future. I came to realize early on that the vision and discipline my mother and her club members had for working with their money are common to many African American women.

Though the history of African American women stretching the dollar is a remarkable one, many still feel that they are doing only a fair or poor job of saving money. I suspect one of the primary reasons for these feelings is the women's unselfish tendency to look after the needs and wants of others first. I've had many women clients tell me that they will begin saving and investing more after they've taken care of their children, husbands, other family members, coworkers, or friends.

This unselfishness is certainly admirable, but I encourage all of my clients to set aside at least a small portion of their weekly earnings—first for an emergency fund and then for retirement investments—so that they can be self-sufficient and reasonably comfortable later in life. Saving and investing are vital to making your money work.

This message is as spiritual as it is practical. I believe our dreams are doorways to the better life that we are all entitled to claim. When you dare to dream, you create a vision for your life. When you write down your dreams, they become goals, and then when you act on goals, they become reality.

Far too many women are reluctant to act on their dreams. They feel guilty, but they shouldn't. On my web site (www.InvestInTheDream.com), I have a list offering hundreds of ways you can cut back on expenses in order to put aside a small portion of your income each week as an investment in your dreams. But first, you have to allow yourself to dream.

Take a few minutes to dream of something you would really, really like to have for yourself Not something practical like a new laptop, a microwave oven, or a wristwatch. I want you to think instead of a really dreamy dream purchase.

Surely you have a secret wish list? Perhaps that diamond necklace you spotted? That family vacation or trip to the Caribbean you've dreamed about for years? How about your dream car? Maybe a new Lexus GS430 with a DVD navigation system? Maybe a comfortable retirement.

Go ahead, indulge your imagination. Dream big! Picture yourself wearing that glittering diamond necklace. Image your grandchildren enjoying Disney World. See yourself shopping, dining, and relaxing in Aruba. Feel the responsiveness of the sleek GS430 on a winding stretch of country road, or the comfort and security of having all your bills paid no matter what life brings.

I work in the pragmatic world of personal finance, but I am a big believer in the power and magic of dreams. I encourage my clients to dream of what they want and then I work with them to build the wealth to live their dreams. You might be amazed to discover that even some of your wildest fantasies are attainable if you simply put some very basic investment principles to work for you.

A great majority of my clients are African American women, and their income levels span a wide range. Some live in penthouse apartments. Others have humble homes in suburbia. Many live in urban communities and earn less than $30,000 a year. No matter what they earn each week, no matter what they may have saved when we first met, through a disciplined and structured savings and investment plan, many have made their dreams come true.

It's possible to build wealth by reevaluating a few simple habits that on the surface look innocent but are contributing to a sabotage of your dreams. Choosing a regular cup of coffee instead of a Double Café Mocha Grande each morning, or skipping the sweet potato pie at lunch, can not only keep you healthy and trim but also help you to realize your dreams as you build wealth to make them a reality.

Did You Get the Message?

Vision and discipline are characteristics basic to many African American women who have successfully managed their financial resources for themselves and their families. See how you measure up when it comes to putting money to work for your and your family's future by answering these statements. Answer True or False to each statement.

1. When allocating money, take care of the essentials first—emergency fund, housing, education, and retirement, but also allow money for your dreams.

2. Dreams are the doorway to the better life that we are all entitled to claim.

3. It is wise to keep your dreams on the back burner. There are more important things to take care of.

4. Unselfish spending on others is admirable, but still set aside a small portion of weekly earnings toward an emergency fund and retirement fund.

5. Many women begin saving and investing after they've taken care of their children, husbands, and other family members.

6. Saving and investing are not vital to making your money work.

7. Many African American families feel that they are doing only a fair or poor job of saving money.

8. There are hundreds of ways you can cut back on expenses in order to put aside a small portion of your income each week.

9. When you write down your dreams, they become goals.

10. When you act on goals, they become reality.

Key

1. T	6. F
2. T	7. T
3. F	8. T
4. T	9. T
5. T	10. T

Chapter 7

INVEST IN YOUR DREAMS

"Nothing ever comes to one that is worth having except as a result of hard work."

—BOOKER T. WASHINGTON

s the following examples illustrate, big dreams can become a reality if you let your money work for you. I encourage you to keep dreaming and learn as much as you can about wise investment practices.

DREAM STORY #1

Tiesha Smith is a twenty-six-year-old single mother who lives on the South Side of Chicago. She is a dynamic young woman determined to escape the poverty of her youth and someday to become a lawyer. Along with taking care of her own seven-year-old son and her mother, who lives in a two-bedroom flat with them, Tiesha works from 8:30 A.M. until 6:30 P.M. (she commutes an hour each way) and then goes to class in pursuit of a bachelor's degree in criminology. She makes about $33,000 a year in her job as a hospital sleep technician, and she gets financial aid for her schooling. As you might imagine, Tiesha does not have a lot of extra spending money lying around, but like most people, she has more wealth-building opportunities than she realizes.

As with all of my clients, I advised Tiesha to first establish a fund for emergencies, and she's done that by having $90 automatically withdrawn from each paycheck and put into a credit-union account. Right now, that is about the extent of her savings. The good news is that she has already started putting money away at a young age in spite of all her expenses and responsibilities as a single mom.

I have a great deal of faith and no little affection for Tiesha. As you can tell, she is a disciplined young sister with solid goals. And she has a dream that you can't help but admire. Her sister Tracy lives in Virginia Beach, Virginia. And Tiesha's fantasy is to move there and purchase her very first house for her son, her mother, and herself

So, let's see if that dream is within her grasp. We'll estimate that the cost of that four-bedroom house will be around $250,000, which seems like a whole lot for a young, single mother, but with a little financial magic, it could be within Tiesha's grasp someday—

let's say within five years. After all, she doesn't have to save the entire amount to buy the house. As a young, first-time home buyer, she will probably need to put only 10 percent of the total down in order to get a mortgage loan.

Tiesha makes about $2,750 a month, or $33,000 a year. If she saved 12 percent of her check—$330—we could put that in an investment account and start building toward a down payment. Assuming that her investments could earn 15 percent a year, in five years she will have her down payment of 10 percent, or about $25,000. Tiesha's dream is achievable if she follows a disciplined savings-and-investment plan to get the down payment and then uses that same discipline to make her house payments. Owning a home is a very worthy dream because, in most parts of the country, houses appreciate in value, and because the interest on a home mortgage is tax deductible. It is actually not just a dream. It is a very wise investment, even though it may seem like a stretch for her at first.

> **The Dream:** A four-bedroom house in Virginia Beach, Virginia
> **Estimated Down Payment:** $25,000
> **Timetable:** 5 years
> **Annual Investment Growth Rate:** 12 percent
> **Systematic Investment Plan for Dream Goal:** Invest $330 every month over a five-year period in an aggressive growth fund with a record of earning at least 15 percent for the last three to five years.

DREAM STORY #2

LaShara Peake is a thirty-one-year-old apprentice pipe fitter for Local 636 in Romulus, Michigan, a suburb of Detroit. When not learning to install heating and cooling systems on construction sites, this attractive and hard-working single mother is caring for her three children ages six, nine, and eleven. Along with her half of the $400 rent on her "too crowded" townhouse shared with her children and a friend, LaShara has to budget at least $500 a month for groceries for her children and $388 for the payments on her 1999 Grand Prix. As an apprentice pipe fitter, she grosses about $35,000 a year. That salary doesn't leave much room for finding her biggest dreams, which include buying her own home someday. So, let's look at one of LaShara's smaller dreams.

Sometime within the next two years, she would like to take a two-week vacation in the Bahamas. "My doctor says I work too hard and I'm stressed out from supporting the kids on my own. I need to go somewhere to get my groove back, just like Stella did," LaShara said. She'd heard from a friend about a package deal for American Airlines and the Port Lucaya Resort and Yacht Club. The total package for airfare from Detroit and 15 nights at the resort is $2,567.10, and of course she'll need at least a little spending money, so let's make it an even $3,000.

LaShara is enrolled in her union's 401(k) retirement plan, although she has not yet fully invested in it. "I have about $7,000 in that I can't touch until retirement. I put the minimum in right now because I'm still an apprentice and I have so many mouths to feed, but I'll probably put in the maximum after I end my apprenticeship next year," she said. I always advise my clients to contribute the maximum amount to their retirement plans, especially when their companies contribute or match funds in it. But I can understand LaShara's decision to hold off until she becomes a full-fledged pipe fitter and begins earning more per hour. She has managed to tuck at least $100 a month away for a special emergency fund, and she told me that she believes she can save another $100 a month for a vacation fund. In two years she would have put away $2,400. If she were able to put it into a fund that paid about 12 percent, through compounding she would have earned about $600, and that would put her over the top. But more than that, she would have developed the discipline of saving, which is the first step to any investment plan.

The Dream: A 15-day vacation in the Bahamas
Estimated Cost: $3,000

Timetable: Bon voyage in two years

Annual Investment Growth Rate: 12 percent

Systematic Investment Plan: Invest $ 100 each month in a growth fund that has a track record of earning at least 12 percent annually for the last five to ten years.

DREAM STORY #3

Kelly Johnson is an exotic, spiritual, and artistic woman who has so many interests and talents she is difficult to define. This forty-something Los Angeles woman has a master's degree in the arts from Columbia College. She is a writer, editor, actress, novelist, and businesswoman with her own multimedia communications consulting company.

Kelly is a big believer in the power of dreams, too, and one of her most enduring desires is to open her own romantic international teahouse. She wants to purchase an older mansion and create a series of tearooms, each one decorated with a different international flavor. She envisions her international house of tea having an English high tea room, a Japanese tearoom, a Hindu tearoom, and an African tearoom, among others.

She believes it would take at least $1 million to get her business up and running through the first year of operation, so she has a five-year timetable for raising the needed funds. Kelly, who is single, has earnings of about $9,000 a month and a 401(k) that has grown to a healthy size, so it should not be difficult for her to realize her dream.

My recommendation is that she tap her savings for a $10,000 initial investment in an aggressive-growth mutual fund that has a history of a 12 percent or better return over a five- to ten-year span. I also suggest that she put away $1,100 a month from her $9,000 monthly net income. That is a little more than 10 percent. I assume inflation will remain low and that she will maintain good credit and be able to get a bank loan or venture capital through a well-written and well-researched business plan. This business plan will lure investors. She will have 10 percent of the money she needs—$100,000—based upon this investment, so that she can easily front the down payment on a bank loan to begin building her dream.

The Dream: A romantic, international house of tearooms in the Los Angeles area

Estimated Cost: $1 million for start-up and first year

Operations: She will need $100,000 for a 10 percent down payment to attract investors or to get a small business loan.

Timetable: Open the doors in the fall of 2006.

Annual Investment Growth Rate: 12 percent

Systematic Investment Plan for Dream Goal: Invest $10,000 in an aggressive-growth mutual fund that has a history of a 12 percent or better return over a five- to ten-year span—and add $1,100 to it each month.

DREAM STORY #4

Nichelle Corbett is a young, upwardly mobile professional woman with an M.B.A. in finance from Howard University and a yearning to travel. Her wanderlust is not surprising, given the fact that as a child Nichelle followed her father as his military career took him to assignments around the United States and Europe.

Nichelle works in Fairfax, Virginia, as a business process improvement consultant with an international accounting firm. She has a very good income and an impressive $1,200-a-month saving habit, most of which goes into her employer's 401(k) plan. Since she is single and without any dependents, Nichelle believes this is a good time to go after her longtime dream of returning to Spain, where she lived as a child. She then would like to cross the Strait of Gibraltar and tour Morocco.

Nichelle has even mapped out an itinerary with her travel agent. Her sixteen-day dream vacation would take her to Madrid, Cordoba, Seville, Jerez, and Ronda in Spain. Then she'd head for Morocco to tour Fez, Meknes, Azrou, Beni Mellal, Marrakech, Ait

Benhaddou, Ouarzazate, and Zagora. She estimates that she would need $4,000 to make her dream come true. Her plan is to invest each week toward her goal so that she can go on her dream trip in four years.

I'd advise Nichelle to begin investing $75 a week in her dream vacation. I'm assuming here that she can invest in a mutual fund that will return at least 12 percent annually, and I've figured in an annual inflation rate of 3 percent. After four years, she should have more than enough to make the journey.

> **The Dream:** A sixteen-day journey to Spain and Africa
> **Estimated Cost:** $4,000
> **Timetable:** Bon voyage in four years
> **Annual Investment Growth Rate:** 12 percent
> **Systematic Investment Plan for Dream Goal:** Invest $75 each week in a growth fund that has a track record of earning at least 12 percent annually for the last five to ten years.

Keep in mind that every investment involves some degree of risk. Your financial health depends on your understanding of what the risks are and knowing how to balance them against the potential rewards. It's one thing to take a calculated risk and quite another to subject your assets to risks that you don't realize you are taking. The primary threat to your savings and investments is the risk of inflation. If your investments cannot keep pace with inflation, your money will lose some of its purchasing power. Stock investments are generally considered among the best ways of addressing inflation risk over the long term. The American economy is in great shape, but many African Americans are turning their dreams into reality each day. Now it's time to take full advantage of your wealth-building capacity.

First, however, there are five things you should know about financial risk:

1. There is no such thing as a risk-free investment. To build assets, you must undertake risk of one kind or another.

2. The greater the risk, the greater the potential reward. However, taking big risks does not necessarily ensure big rewards. You must know the risks and weigh them against the possible rewards. The bottom line: Reasonable risk equals reasonable reward.

3. Make sure you are comfortable with the risk level of the investments you choose. If you can't sleep, then the risk is too great.

4. Manage risk—don't try to escape it. Instead, diversify your investments, invest over time to offset market fluctuations, and monitor your accounts to ensure that the risk/reward parameters you have set have not changed.

5. Maintain a long-term horizon. Holding mutual funds over a long period eases out volatility.

Prosperity is a skill that can be practiced and learned just like balancing your checkbook or mastering a new language. The first step is to imagine what you want for your life and then to begin taking steps toward your goal. Your ability to save and invest money has less to do with how much you make than with how you manage it. The road to prosperity can begin with just one dollar a day if wisely leveraged. So, tap into this country's strong economy and use its power to build lasting wealth. And remember that dreams that are worth your dreaming are dreams that are worth investing in.

Did You Get the Message?

Most of us have more wealth-building opportunities than we realize. By starting to put money away at any age in spite of all our expenses and responsibilities, we are developing the discipline of saving, which is the first step toward any investment plan. Are you ready to take your first step? Answer True or False to each statement.

1. Big dreams can become a reality if you let your money work for you.

2. There is no such thing as a risk-free investment. To build assets, you must undertake risk of one kind or another.

3. You don't have to be comfortable with the risk level of the investments you choose.

4. Diversifying your investments will help you manage risk.

5. Ignoring market fluctuations will help you manage risk.

6. Managing risk is impossible.

7. Holding mutual funds over a long period eases out volatility.

8. Buying a house is a very wise investment because it will usually appreciate in value.

9. It's not a good idea to contribute the maximum amount to your retirement plans, especially when your employer contributes or matches funds to it.

10. Stock investments are generally considered among the best ways of addressing inflation risk over the long term.

Key

1. T		6. F	
2. T		7. T	
3. F		8. T	
4. T		9. F	
5. F		10. T	

Chapter 8

TO SUCCEED FINANCIALLY, IT'S OKAY TO BE SELFISH

"If you keep on doing what you are doing, you are going to keep on getting what you get, so if you don't like what you've been getting, you should look at what you've been doing. Prosperity is your birthright."

—LES BROWN
Author/Public Speaker, The Motivator

Y ou would be hard pressed to convince me that there isn't a person who does not need at least some of his or her money in a retirement portfolio or savings plan.

I know all the arguments: "I need the income now!" "I'm too old to start saving now, I need all the money I earn to live off of now." "Anyway, I have Social Security benefits." I would counter by saying that I don't know anyone who knows when he or she will retire or can confidently tell me that all retirement costs are provided for. I know very few people who do not wish to leave a financial legacy to their heirs. Finally, I have never met anyone opposed to increasing their income!

Like it or not, medical science is keeping people alive longer. It wasn't too many years ago that we envisioned seventy-five-year-old people sitting in chairs, rocking away their final years. When I see seventy-five-year-old people today, they're involved in all types of activities. Extended longevity has changed our view on planning for our future. Money has to play a role in how we see our future. More years on the planet means the necessity for more money. So, let's look at some ways in which money affects our future.

First, let's talk about demographics. The United States has been accused of being a nation of slackers. When it comes to saving money, we undersave, compared to the rest of the world.

Now, look at this picture from a different angle. In the eighteen years following the end of World War II, millions of babies were born in the United States. Those babies are now turning fifty years old. Having raised a child, I submit that it's pretty darn difficult to save money before age forty-five. We don't buy sneakers, we buy Reeboks and Nikes. Name-brand-this and name-brand-that begin to add up, as do car payments, mortgage payments, and college tuition.

Next, let's look at the investment argument. During a recent period, the stock market was up 250 percent. In one or two memorable days, it was down 24 percent. Since 1940, we've had twelve bull markets (stocks on a general incline in value) in this country. The average bull market lasted over three years and was up 100 percent. In the same time frame, we've seen eleven bear markets (stocks on a general decline in value). The average bear market lasted less than a year and was down 25–30 percent. When looked at rationally, the stock market is a wonderful place to be. The puzzlement is that more African Americans don't take advantage of it.

My experience has been that, sometimes, we as African Americans don't appreciate or understand volatility (the ups and downs of the market) and it frightens us as a result. We treat liquidity (keeping cash) like our best friend, when in fact liquidity is both expensive and disruptive to the best plans.

One thousand dollars in treasury bills bought forty years ago is worth $7,200 today. The same $1,000 invested in the stock market is worth $109,000. Yet when the top thirty-four months of market action are removed from these astounding market results, the $1,000 in the stock market is worth only $6,900, less than treasury bills! Anyone who thinks he can pick the 3½ weeks a year when the market's action takes place is deceiving himself.

The only alternative to market timing is dollar cost averaging. Dollar cost averaging has only two requirements: patience and a fundamental belief in the continued prosperity of the American system. First of all, the greatest single obstacle to financial success in the United States today is lack of patience. Second, anyone who has ever placed his faith in the American system has always been right.

The well-known economist Roger Ibbotson tells us that "if we had invested a dollar back in 1925, because of inflation that $1.00 would today be worth $7.46. In government bonds, today's value would be $17.99. If we had invested in corporate bonds, we'd have $27.18 today. But in the stock market, we'd have $517.50. What we need to be reminded is that only $25.89 of the $517.50 can be credited to price appreciation." The balance came about only because of dividend growth and dividend reinvestment. This is the best reason for buying and holding equity securities. The key to investment success is time, not timing.

Let me use the a typical mutual fund as an example. A $10,000 investment in August 1961, at 12 percent would be worth in excess of $1,200,000 on a fully reinvested basis. On the same terms over the same time period, a savings account would be worth less than $50,000 at 4 percent.

Savings accounts and certificates of deposit are not better than mutual funds. A retirement savings plan is the best investment method.

If you work for a city, state, or county, there is no better way to invest for retirement than with a tax-deferred savings program.

The IRS 457 savings plan is a program provided by a government employer who establishes a Deferred Compensation Plan under the Internal Revenue Code for government employees or a 401(k) plan for employees of a private for-profit corporation or small business. A nonprofit organization can set up a 403(b) tax-deferred savings or annuity plan providing a variable benefit for the employee. The plan makes it possible for you to defer income and the payment of income taxes on the deferred amounts. This money is then placed in a tax-deferred investment of your choice, selected from those made available under the plan.

1. All contributions are tax deferred until withdrawn from the plan (CD investments are made with after-tax dollars and taxed every year whether you can get to the money or not).
2. All growth, dividends or interest, is deferred from taxes until withdrawn from the plan (all other investments are taxed annually except IRAs).
3. You can defer up to $8,000 annually into a savings plan (depending on government regulations) if you work for the government (even if you choose an IRA, it would be funded with "after-tax" dollars and would be limited to $2,000). If you work for a nonprofit organization, your tax-sheltered annuity will allow you to save $9,500 or more. You can save even more with a 401(k) from a privately held company.

4. All monies contributed to a savings plan are deducted from your W-2 income, therefore lowering your taxable income each year.

The purpose of the plan is to provide a convenient method of accumulating money for future use to meet your objectives. For example, you should be concerned about:

1. Increasing your financial independence
2. Supplementing your retirement income
3. Providing a possible hedge against inflation in future years
4. Accumulating more money than is usually possible using conventional "after-tax" savings methods, and/or
5. Reducing your current income-tax liability

The IRS 457 plan is not intended for savings and investments of a short-term nature, since monies deferred are generally not available unless you terminate employment or retire. African Americans in the following categories should seriously investigate the benefits of the plan:

1. Generally, those who are paying substantial amounts of income taxes
2. Families or individuals with multiple incomes
3. Single persons with no dependents
4. Those concerned with having a comfortable retirement
5. Those currently saving or investing with after-tax dollars
6. People who overwithhold and use their tax refund as a forced-savings device

ANSWERS TO QUESTIONS YOU MAY HAVE

The following description of the IRS 457 plan has been prepared to help you understand its mechanics and answer some of the most common questions. It should, however, be read in conjunction with the complete text of the plan document. Your employer will select a mutual fund or insurance company as the investment vehicle. That company will select a plan representative. Your plan representative will be available to answer your personal questions and explain the plan as it might apply to you.

1. WHAT IS DEFERRED COMPENSATION?

The Deferred Compensation Plan consists of a written agreement between you and your employer. This agreement provides for the deferral of a specified amount of your before-tax dollars for investment. Such deferred amounts and all earnings, less any applicable charges, will be paid to you at a later date, usually when you are retired and probably in a lower tax bracket. The amount deferred is not included on your W-2 for income-tax purposes during the year in which it is earned. Deferred income is taxable only at the time of distribution. The amount of tax you pay depends upon how much total income you receive in each calendar year during the withdrawal period. Your total income for a given calendar year will include any payments received as benefits from your deferred compensation account during that year.

2. WHAT HAPPENS TO THE AMOUNTS DEFERRED?

When you request that your employer defer a portion of your compensation, you also request that your employer invest the deferred income in one or several of the investment options available under the plan that you have personally selected.

3. WHAT IS THE BENEFIT TO ME?

The benefit of a deferred compensation plan lies in the fact that income taxes are imposed only upon the earnings that you actually receive during the year. By deferring receipt of a portion of your compensation, you postpone the payment of income tax and gain investment earnings on the money you would have otherwise paid in taxes. The law permits the delay of payment of tax on both the deferrals and any gain on the investment until you actually receive distributions from your account. Instead of losing a portion of each dollar earned to taxes, you can now invest up to 25 percent of your annual earnings in a tax-deferred account (to a maximum of $8,000 per year). Your income taxes for the year will be based on the income remaining after your deferral.

4. Can You Give Me an Example?

For the sake of illustration, let us assume that Mary Jones is currently saving $50 per pay period from her take-home pay of $467. By enrolling in the Deferred Compensation Plan, Mary is able to save $62 per pay period—an increase of 24 percent in savings—and still have the same take-home pay! The chart below shows this advantage.

Table 8.1
Deferred vs. Nondeferred Savings Advantages

Without Deferred Compensation		With Deferred Compensation
$600	Gross Salary	$600
-0-	Pretax savings	$ 62
$600	Taxable Income	$538
$ 83	Taxes*	$ 71
$517	After-tax Dollars	$467
$ 50	After-tax Savings	$ -0-
$467	Take Home	$467

* Includes state and federal taxes, claiming married, and no dependents

The following accumulation table shows the long-term benefit to Mary of saving with pre-tax dollars through the Deferred Compensation Plan.

TABLE 8.2
Savings Accumulation

Without Deferred Compensation		With Deferred Compensation
$1,300 annually/$50 biweekly		$1,612 annually/$62 biweekly
$ 18,023	10 years	$ 24,286
$ 52,816	20 years	$ 76,718
$ 116,235	30 years	$ 189,914

*Assumes a marginal 20 percent combined tax bracket and an average 8 percent interest projection

5. WHO IS ELIGIBLE TO PARTICIPATE AND WHEN?

All officers and employees of IRS 457, 401(k), and 403(b) plan participating companies are eligible to participate in the plan. Deferrals cannot begin until the month after you execute a participation agreement that instructs your employer to defer a portion of your compensation.

Your plan representative can tell you the pay period during which deferrals will begin.

6. IS THERE A LIMIT TO THE AMOUNT THAT MAY BE DEFERRED?

Yes. Generally you may set aside up to 25 percent of your gross compensation from your employer during any tax year up to a maximum of $8,000. The dollar maximum will increase with the cost-of-living adjustment allowance by the federal government through legislation each year. The most important changes affecting IRS 457 plans are:

1. Plan assets are now to be held in a separate trust, entrusted by the employer, for the "exclusive benefit" of participants

and their beneficiaries. In the past, plan assets were held as assets of employers, available to general creditors in the case of bankruptcy.

2. Plan participants are allowed one time change in electing when benefits will begin. The old irrevocable election is now enhanced to allow one change in timing as long as benefit payments have not yet begun and the date for benefits to begin is no earlier than the original date.

3. *De minimus* in-service distributions may be made. Beginning in 1998, account balances may be paid out to participants prior to termination as long as the balance is less than $3,500, no contributions have been made for the last 24 months, and no prior distributions have been made under this provision.

In addition, employees who have not deferred their maximum amount in previous years may, during the last three taxable years ending prior to the year in which they retire, "catch up" on the deferrals they were eligible to set aside but did not, to a maximum of $15,000 per year with no percentage limitation. Even if they did not participate at all previously, the "catch-up" rule still applies!

7. Is There a Minimum Amount For Deferral?

Yes. You may defer as little as $10 per pay period to any single investment option.

8. Must All Deferrals Be Payroll Deducted?

Yes. However, individuals who wish to make a maximum deferral but don't enroll until later in the year can raise their contribution level above the 25 percent limit in order to reach the annual maximum. Theoretically, an individual who wanted to transfer money into the plan from a taxable savings account could agree to a maximum deferral, then take whatever was needed from the taxable account to supplement their take-home pay.

9. CAN I INCREASE OR DECREASE THE AMOUNT OF MY DEFERRAL?

Yes, twice per year during the scheduled reenrollment periods for the plan, and, if necessary, at other times upon request. The change will become effective within six weeks. Such changes must be performed by a plan representative. They may not be made directly with your employer's payroll department.

10. CAN I CHANGE INVESTMENT OPTIONS?

Yes. You can redirect your deferrals to a different investment at any time either with your plan representative or by mail. You may also transfer past deferrals from one investment to another. There are restrictions to the transfer privileges from the "fixed"-rate investments, which you should discuss with your plan representative.

11. CAN I STOP CONTRIBUTING TO THE PLAN?

Yes. You may stop or start deferrals at any time by executing a financial change form with your plan representative. Such changes will be effective in the month following your request.

12. CAN I GET MY MONEY BACK AT ANY TIME?

No. According to IRS regulations, account values are payable if you die, become disabled, terminate employment, or retire. The only exception to this rule, while you are still employed, is for an unforeseeable financial emergency under the financial hardship provision of the plan.

13. WHAT CONSTITUTES AN UNFORESEEABLE EMERGENCY?

Emergencies requiring normally unbudgetable funds are considered "unforeseeable." Expenses (such as school tuition or the purchase of a car or house) and minor emergencies (such as car repair, appliance replacement, or other normal upkeep and maintenance) are not considered unforeseeable emergencies by the IRS.

The employer emergency withdrawal officer or committee will use the standards of the IRS to determine if an unforeseeable emergency exists.

If you suffer an unforeseeable emergency that is not satisfied by stopping deferrals, you may apply for a withdrawal of the portion of your account value to meet this need.

14. Who Owns My Deferred Compensation Funds?

Technically, your employer, being tax-exempt, owns the funds. However, you have your employer's written agreement to pay the proceeds of your account to you (or your beneficiaries). In recent years a federal law has established a trust arrangement for the employees whereby the plan can be a trust set aside for the benefit of the employees. The trust arranger thereby gives the employees added security that the monies set aside in the plan would be used for the exclusive benefit of the participants and their beneficiaries. The monies set aside can be used in case of retirement, termination of employment, qualifying financial emergency, disability, or death. If you were to own the funds in your name, the amounts deferred and all earnings on them would be currently taxable to you.

15. May I Use These Funds As Collateral?

No. Deferred compensation funds are not assignable as collateral. Neither are they subject to judgments or attachments, since they are technically not yours until distributed to you.

16. What Happens If I Terminate Employment or Retire?

Within 60 days after separation of service, you are required to make an irrevocable election as to the distribution of your account. You may either begin withdrawal immediately or postpone withdrawal until a future date, usually retirement age.

1. If you choose to postpone withdrawal, your account will continue to accumulate earnings in a tax-sheltered environment.
2. When you begin withdrawal of your account, it will be paid to you in one, or a combination, of the following ways:
   - a lump sum
   - monthly, quarterly, or annual payments over a specified period of years
   - a lifetime income through an annuity, with all the standard variations: life, life with "period certain," or joint survivor.

Federal taxes are withheld from all distributions.

17. What Happens If I Die Before Receiving a Distribution?

Your beneficiaries are entitled to the full value of your account. They have the same rights as you in deciding how these benefits will be distributed. However, if your beneficiary is not your spouse, he or she must elect a payout option that will distribute the account in 15 years or less.

18. When Will I Have to Pay Income Taxes?

Your income taxes will be payable the year or years in which your accumulated deferred compensation account is paid out to you or your beneficiaries. Taxes are assessed only on the amounts actually paid to you in any tax year.

19. Does This Guarantee That I Will Pay Less In Taxes?

Most of us can expect to have less taxable income and to be taxed at lower rates during retirement than when we are working. The major increase in the standard deduction contained in TRA '86 for individuals or couples over 65 and the "indexing" of the personal deduction amount to inflation strongly contribute to this probability. If this proves to be true in your case, you would pay much less in taxes; however, it cannot be guaranteed.

20. Does The Deferred Compensation Plan Affect My Pension Benefits?

No. Your pension benefits are not changed in any way.

21. Does The Deferred Compensation Plan Affect Social Security Benefits?

No. Social Security benefits for which you may be eligible are not affected in any way.

22. Will Periodic Reports Be Made to Me?

Yes. You will be provided with a quarterly statement showing the status of all your deferrals plus investment earnings, less any applicable charges.

23. Are There Any Costs That Are included?

It depends entirely upon the investment options available under the plan. Participants in stock, bond, and money-market accounts will be charged a management fee that is described in the respective prospectuses. Any other attendant fees, if applicable, will be detailed in the investment product literature. Ask your plan representative to explain what charges, if any, may apply.

Did You Get the Message?

Many African Americans have, admittedly, not considered the fact that because of medical science, we are living longer, and that we need to save now for our retirement. Hopefully, you have taken note on the subject and are ready to test your knowledge about saving for the future. Answer True or False to each statement.

1. On average, there are more bull markets in stock-market history and they last longer than bear markets.

2. Dollar cost averaging has only two requirements, patience and a fundamental belief in the continued prosperity of the American system.

3. A strong economy depends on a solid campaign by the federal government and lots of money invested.

4. If you work for a city, state, or county, there is no better way to invest for retirement than with a tax-deferred savings program.

5. The IRA retirement plan is not intended for savings and investments of a short-term nature.

6. When you invest in an IRA retirement plan, you can get your money back any time you want.

7. Liquidity is both expensive and disruptive to the best plans.

8. The greatest single obstacle to financial success in the United States today is lack of patience.

9. Savings accounts and certificates of deposits are better than mutual funds.

10. A retirement savings plan is the best investment method.

Key

1. T		6. F	
2. T		7. T	
3. F		8. T	
4. T		9. F	
5. T		10. T	

Chapter 9

FIFTY MONEY-SAVING TIPS TO HELP YOU GET STARTED

"The important thing is not how much money a person makes; it is what he does with it that matters."

—A. G. GASTON
Entrepreneur

Now, with a little help from one of the 9,000 mutual-fund families, I would like to give you 50 practical ways to save $50 each month. Saving money doesn't have to be difficult. In fact, if you take a close look at how you're spending your monthly income, you'll be surprised at just how easy it is to cut expenses. After all, the best way to save money is to spend less of what you make. Here's a list of 50 money-saving tips to help get you started:

1. Shop with a list—and stick to it.
2. Just say *no* to ATMs with fees—plan ahead for your cash needs.
3. Does your bank charge high fees? *Move your account.*
4. Pay off that credit-card balance!
5. If you must carry a credit-card balance, shop around for a card with a lower rate.
6. Look for lower premiums on your insurance policies.
7. Consider higher deductibles for your home and auto insurance.
8. Do you have private mortgage insurance? If you've built up 20 percent equity in your home, you can cancel it.
9. Use a mail-order pharmacy for long-term prescription use.
10. "Doc, can I get that as a generic drug?"
11. Check all medical and hospital bills for errors—many insurance companies offer rewards.
12. Rent—never buy something you'll only use a few times.
13. Turn your yard into a department store—have a rummage sale.
14. Switch long-distance carriers—then switch again.
15. Call waiting? Not usually? Cancel those add-on phone services you don't need.
16. E-mail your friends instead of calling.
17. Skip the movies—rent a video instead.
18. Dine out? Eat in.
19. Lunch is "in the bag"—or it should be.

20. Don't buy that book! Exercise your library card (you need to buy my book, though!).

21. Free up space in your mailbox—cancel that subscription to a magazine you never read.

22. Watch a parade or have a picnic—free entertainment is often the best.

23. Turn your car into a "chat room." Carpool to work.

24. Join the "bus crowd" and avoid cab fare.

25. Buy airline tickets in advance—and always stay through Saturday. You'll have more fun, and it's a lot cheaper, too!

26. Quit that health club—join the local gym instead.

27. "Coupons" and "double-coupon days." Enough said.

28. What's in a name? Buy generic instead.

29. Skip the paper towels—wash your cloth ones instead.

30. Watch out for "convenience" foods—they're expensive and not as healthy for you anyway.

31. Join a warehouse club.

32. "Scan" those scanners and receipts—mistakes do happen.

33. Avoid "pricey" specialty stores.

34. Comparison shop "online."

35. Got a trunk? Buy in bulk.

36. Premium gas for your car? Most run fine without it. Check your owner's manual to be sure.

37. Forget the words "automatic car-wash." Do it yourself and get some fresh air.

38. Use that quick-change oil-and-lube service on the corner instead of a full-service garage.

39. Never pay extra for service contracts or extended warranties—the manufacturer's warranty is usually sufficient.

40. Cancel that premium channel you never watch—or cancel cable TV altogether.

41. Don't touch that thermostat—put on a sweater instead.

42. Take a shower instead of a bath.

43. Run only a "full" dishwasher.

44. Have an energy audit done on your home—some companies offer them for *free.*
45. Never pay extra for car rental insurance—you're probably already covered by your credit card or regular car insurance.
46. *Don't play the lottery*—the odds of getting hit by lightning are better than your chances of winning.
47. Time to refinance your home? Keep an eye on interest rates.
48. Pay yourself first—set aside a dollar a day.
49. Buy a "piggy bank" for all the spare change you keep finding in your couch.
50. Don't spend your next pay raise—INVEST THAT MONEY INSTEAD.

By putting away $2 a day you should be able to save at least $50 a month. If you are twenty-five years old and you invest that money until you are sixty-five, you would have saved $24,000. If you had invested in today's average mutual fund at a reasonable 12 percent rate of return, you would have over $600,000 in your account for retirement.

Let me be very specific. Here's an actual growth-and-income mutual fund as an example. A $10,000 investment on July 1, 1961, would have been worth in excess of $1,200,000 as of June 30, 2001, on a fully reinvested basis. On the same terms over the same time period, a savings account would have been worth less than $50,000.

Did You Get the Message?

We should all take a close look at how we're spending our monthly income. As African Americans, it's conceivable that, because of various logistics, we are probably charged more for many of life's necessities, but let's see if you've got a grasp on the basics. Answer True or False to each statement.

1. Getting higher deductibles for your home and auto insurance can help you save money.

2. If your bank charges high fees, you should move your account.

3. If you get a raise, invest.

4. If you get a windfall, spend it.

5. If you receive an income-tax refund, give it to friends.

6. When buying a home, the last thing you should think about are interest rates.

7. Shopping with a list and sticking to it will help you save money.

8. The best way to save money is to spend less of what you make.

9. Always pay extra for car-rental insurance.

10. Never pay extra for service contracts or extended warranties.

Key

1. T		6. F	
2. T		7. T	
3. T		8. T	
4. F		9. F	
5. F		10. T	

Chapter 10

MONEY-MAKING STRATEGIES THAT WORK FOR EVERYONE

"Some people succeed because they are destined to, but most people succeed because they are determined to."

—ROSCOE DUNJEE

Activist

ccording to a recent poll, only 6 out of 10 Americans list a steady source of retirement income as their primary financial goal. So you're not alone if you have overlooked this area in the past. Most people find it difficult to plan for events that are 30 or 40 years into the future. Regardless of this fact, security in your retirement years is available if you have the desire, discipline and a little basic knowledge. At this point, you've already learned a great deal.

Now it's time to combine what you've learned with a few more additional strategies that can make a tremendous difference in your retirement accumulation.

For many African Americans, there are five possible sources of retirement income. Let's take a look at these sources and the estimated percentages they may lend toward your retirement income.

TABLE 10.1
Retirement Income

Source	Percentage
Personal Savings and Investments	39%
Pension	15%
Employment	23%
Social Security	20%
Other	3%

Source: U.S. Department of Commerce

LEARNING HOW TO MAXIMIZE YOUR PERSONAL SAVINGS

In the previous chapters, we've discussed the impact of four very important building blocks for maximizing your savings: time, consistency, rate of return and compound interest. The next logical step is to take action to put these ideas into practice.

Just like all other aspects of your life, the responsibility of planning for your retirement is yours. There are good reasons this responsibility lies in your hands. Remember our discussion about the "Baby Boomers?" In the mid-50s, there were 7.3 workers for every Social Security retiree. Instead of the numbers of workers increasing in the mid-90s, it has instead decreased to 4.8 workers. It is currently estimated by the year 2030, when the "Baby Boomers" reach retirement, that number will be reduced even further—to 2.8 workers. We are faced with the likelihood that Social Security will be defunct at a time when more individuals will be expecting to receive benefits. This means that the other sources of retirement income will have to increase their share.

Most companies, in today's economic environment, are providing their workers with defined contribution programs, such as 401(k)'s. They are shifting the burden and responsibility of retirement to the individual. This means today's workers have to be more savvy in their planning by understanding the positive and negative aspects of how they save their money.

Remember your parents being hired at a job and knowing they could keep it for life? In our competitive world where other countries are providing incentives for American companies to relocate, jobs for Americans are no longer guaranteed. This leaves the opportunity to build a pension plan in limbo.

Because of these three factors, most people are gradually facing the reality that financial self-reliance is a way of life.

At least 86% of all Americans realize they can only rely on their own skills and abilities if they are going to be successful in today's world. In 1984, only 75% of all Americans believed this to be true.

There is still a gap in the understanding of what these figures mean for the average individual. We know the gap exists because retirement savings continue to decline, rather than increase.

You've learned some pretty frightening statistics, but you can use this information to your advantage if you grasp the most important factor in this discussion about maximizing your savings: The best way to ensure adequate retirement income is to maximize your personal savings.

Inflation—Another Stake in the Heart of Your Plan

When the price or value of an article is raised above it's real value, we consider it inflated. This inflation can adversely affect every aspect of your financial game plan. The inflation rate has stayed below 5 percent since 1990, but even if it remains low, it will still have some type of effect on your savings or investment. Consider if you only earn a 4 percent rate of return on your savings or investment plan, and inflation is 5 percent. You are already losing money. In order for your savings to grow, it's smart to look for a rate of return that's higher than the current inflation rate.

Everyone is aware that their dollar doesn't purchase as much as it did in the past. This decline in the dollar's purchasing power is mainly due to inflation.

When you look at your assets in this context, the loss of purchasing power can be significant. If you earned $25,000 in 1971, you needed $19,000 more in 1981 to make the same purchases. By 1991 you needed $41,332, due once again to a 5 percent inflation rate. If you want to maintain the same purchasing power beginning in the year 2001, you will need $83,048. These are startling facts, but they give you a better idea of how crucial the rate of inflation is to your finances.

Tax Shelters

Anyone who has a job or buys a product pays some type of tax. How many times have you worked overtime and seen a large portion of the extra dollars go toward taxes? The more you work, the more taxes you pay. It's just that simple. It stands to reason, then, that in order to have the most cash possible at retirement, you need to find some way to minimize the taxes you pay.

When you hear the term tax shelter, what type of people come to mind? It's normally someone wealthy. But, actually, we all have the same access to tax shelters as the wealthy. Most often the average American just isn't aware of where to look or how to go about setting one up.

In the early 1980s, Congress passed a law than enabled every working American under 70½ years of age to make contributions to an IRA, Individual Retirement Account.

IRAs are one of the best tax shelters available. Let's discuss some of the new IRAs and the ways they can save you money each year.

Congress created two new IRAs in 1998—the Roth IRA and the Education IRA. It also made changes to the traditional IRAs. The Traditional Nondeductible IRA is an account where contributions are not deductible, but investments can grow and be tax-deferred until they are withdrawn.

If you are married and your adjusted gross income is more than $160,000, and you are under age 70½, you can invest the lesser of $2,000 or what you earned in a nondeductible IRA. The same applies to a single person with an adjusted gross income of more than $100,000. In addition, this IRA doesn't affect your participation in a retirement plan at work.

The traditional deductible IRA is an account where contributions are deductible against your taxable income and your investment can grow tax-deferred until withdrawn. Just like the nondeductible IRA, you must be under age 70½ in order to contribute to this IRA. Even if your spouse doesn't work but participates in a retirement plan, if your joint adjusted gross income is less than $150,000, you can still invest up to $2,000 in his or her IRA as long as your joint earnings are at least $2,000.

This means if you are in the 35 percent tax bracket (a combination of 28 percent federal and 7 percent state tax), you could save $700 in one year merely by starting an IRA. Taking it one step further, if your earnings are tax-deferred until retirement, you will be using these funds at a time when you are likely to be in a lower tax bracket. When viewed from this aspect, your IRA could be an excellent vehicle for long-term savings.

The Roth IRA is one in which the contributions are not deductible, but your investment can grow tax-free. In addition "qualified" withdrawals are tax-free. This means any taxpayer of any age with an earned income of $2,000 or more can invest up to a maximum of $2,000 annually per person in a Roth IRA if your modified adjusted gross income is less than $150,000 for a married couple filing jointly or $95,000 for a single person. Bear in mind that a modified adjusted income is one that excludes foreign earned income, foreign housing deductions, IRA deductions, and/or Series EE bond interest reported on Form 8815.

You can take your earnings out tax-free and penalty-free after you have had the Roth IRA for at least five years, but you must have satisfied one of the following requirements:

1. You must have reached 59½.
2. You must have a qualifying disability.
3. You have received benefits as a beneficiary.
4. Your proceeds must be used for a first-home purchase up to $10,000 during your lifetime.

The Education IRA allows a parent, grandparent, or relative to contribute up to $500 per year to be used for college for each child under the age of 18. Only one education IRA can be set up for each minor child. The contributions are nondeductible, but withdrawals for college expenses such as tuition, room and board, books, fees and supplies will not be taxed. The money in this IRA has to be spent before the child turns age 30 or it will be taxed and a 10 percent penalty will apply.

You can establish this IRA if your modified adjusted gross income as a married person is less than $150,000, or $95,000 if you are single. Even if the parent doesn't qualify, the grandparents or relative may qualify.

WHICH IS BEST—DEDUCTION OR DEFERRAL?

In terms of your gross income, a deduction is money you subtract before you calculate taxes. When you can reduce your gross income with deductions, you'll have to pay less in income tax. On the other hand, if you defer, or postpone payment of current taxes until retirement, you are likely to be in a lower tax bracket when you do have to pay taxes.

Even though the Tax Reform Act of 1986 made a few changes, it didn't restrict the ability to defer the payment of taxes until retirement. So, in terms of long-term income building, deferral is far more important than deductibility. Just remember to take advantage of every deduction or deferral you can.

NEW LEGISLATION FROM THE IRS

In August of 1997, the Internal Revenue Service changed some rulings that positively affected IRAs. One of those changes was the establishment of the HOPE Scholarship Credit and the Lifetime Learning Credit. Because these changes are so complex, I'd suggest you contact your tax adviser to determine what new rulings affect you. After that is accomplished, you should talk with your financial adviser as well.

These new rules began to broaden the opportunities for investors in the areas of tax-free earnings, education IRAs to help fund your child's education, penalty-free distributions for what is termed "lifestyle purchases," increased opportunities for deductible IRAs, and new rollover opportunities.

The following charts will help you understand the new legislation and its impact by comparing the traditional IRA and the two new IRAs created with the 1997 legislation.

To determine how new legislation might impact your financial plan, or what kind of IRA is best for you, remember to consult your tax adviser, financial planner, or attorney.

Table 10.2   IRA Comparision Charts

PROVISION	PRESENT LAW	TAXPAYER RELIEF ACT
Traditional IRA		
In General	An individual may make annual deductible IRA contributions up to the lesser of $2,000 or the amount of the individual's compensation if the individual (or his or her spouse) is not an active participant in an employer-sponsored qualified retirement plan.	The individual would be "decoupled" from his or her spouse so that the spouse's participation in an employer-sponsored plan will not affect the individual's ability to make deductible contributions to an IRA, as long as the spouse's joint income is less than $150,000. (Effective after 1997.)
Income Phaseout Range	If the individual (or his or her spouse) is an active qualified retirement plan participant, the $2,000 limit on deductible contributions is phased out between $40,000 and $50,000 of adjusted gross income for married couples, and between $25,000 and $35,000 of AGI for single individuals.	The income limits for eligibility to make deductible IRA contributions where the individual is an active participant would be increased over time, beginning in 1998 until the phaseout range reaches $80,000 to $100,000 of adjusted gross income for married couples (in the year 2007), and $50,000 and $60,000 income for single individuals (in the year 2005). The contribution limit will phase out if the individual's spouse is an active participant in a plan and their joint income exceeds $150,000.
Overall Limit on Deductible Plan Contributions	Currently, deductible contributions made to an IRA are not counted toward the annual limit on total deductible contributions to qualified plans under Section 402(b).	No change from present law.
Spousal IRAs	The annual limit for each spouse (regardless of whether the spouse has an income) is $2,000, but the couple's aggregate deductible contributions may not exceed the combined compensation of both spouses.	The annual limit for each spouse (regardless of whether the spouse has an income) is $2,000, but the couple's aggregate deductible contributions may not exceed the combined compensation of both spouses plus any contributions to a Roth IRA.
Waiver of Section 27(t) Penalty	A 10% early-withdrawal penalty applies to any distribution taken before the individual reaches age 59½ unless the distribution is on account of death or disability, is made in the form of periodic payments after separation from service, or is made for a "Special Purpose" (i.e., certain medical expenses or unemployment).	Same as present law, but in addition: no withdrawal penalty for distributions for first-time home purchases or higher education expenses, including tuition, fees, books, supplies, and equipment required for attendance at eligible higher educational institutions or certain vocational education schools. (Effective for distributions after 12/31/97 with respect to expenses paid after that date for education in academic periods beginning after that date.)

PROVISION	PRESENT LAW	TAXPAYER RELIEF ACT

Nondeductible Roth IRA

In General	While present law permits individuals to make nondeductible contributions (up to $2,000) to a Traditional IRA to the extent the individual cannot (or does not elect to) make deductible contributions, the earnings on such nondeductible contributions are taxable when withdrawn.	Individuals would be permitted to make annual contributions to a Roth IRA, subject to the limits described below, and contributions and earnings may be withdrawn tax free in certain circumstances (effective after 1997).
Income Limits on Eligibility to Contribute	No income limitation on eligibility to make nondeductible contributions.	The full contribution amount for a Roth IRA is phased out between $150,000 and $160,000 (for married couples) and $95,000 and $110,000 (for single individuals).
Over Limits on Plan Contributions	Nondeductible contributions to IRAs are not currently affected by the amount of elective deferrals made to a 401(k) plan or 403(b) program.	Same as present law, but contributions made to a Traditional IRA are counted toward the annual limit on contributions to a Roth IRA. The maximum contribution to a Roth IRA is $2,000 ($4,000 per married couple) less contributions to all IRAs other than to a Roth IRA.
Distributions	Contributions are returned tax free but earnings are taxable. Distributions prior to age 59½ are subject to an early withdrawal penalty unless the distribution is due to death or disability, made in periodic payments, for certain medical expenses or on account of unemployment.	All amounts (including the earnings) may be withdrawn tax free and without application of the 10% early withdrawal penalty if (1) a 5-year holding requirement is satisfied; and (2) the withdrawal is made after the individual attains age 59½, dies, becomes disabled, or amounts are used for a first-time home purchase for the individual or certain family members. Other distributions are taxable to the extent of earnings and subject to the 10% early withdrawal penalty rules.
Five-Year Holding Period	No provision.	The five-year holding period would begin to run with respect to all contributions (and their earnings) made to a Roth IRA on January 1 of the year in which the first contribution is made to the Roth IRA. As a result, the five-year period would begin with the first year for which the Roth IRA is opened. For rollover contributions from a Traditional IRA, the five-year period will begin with the year of rollover.

PROVISION	PRESENT LAW	TAXPAYER RELIEF ACT
Nondeductible Roth IRA continued		
Ordering Rule	No provision.	For purposes of determining what portion of a distribution is taxable earnings where the five-year holding requirement and the special purpose requirement are not both met, distributions would be treated as made from contributions first. As a result, no portion of a distribution would be treated as taxable earnings until the total distribution amount exceeds the total amount of contributions.
Rollovers	No provision.	A Roth IRA may be rolled over to another Roth IRA tax free. If the taxpayer's adjusted gross income does not exceed $100,000, amounts held in a Traditional IRA may be rolled over into a Roth IRA; however, the individual will be immediately taxed on the amount rolled over. If such rollover occurs before January 1, 1999, the tax can be paid over a four-year period, beginning with the year of the rollover. The 10% early withdrawal tax will not apply to amounts rolled over.
Contributions after age 70½	Not permitted.	An individual may contribute to a Roth IRA after age 70½.
Distributions after 70½	Required minimum distributions must begin after the calendar year in which taxpayer attains age 70½, and also must be made after a taxpayer's death.	No minimum distributions required prior to death. The post-death minimum distribution rules under Section 401(a)(9) continue to apply.

PROVISION	PRESENT LAW	TAXPAYER RELIEF ACT
Education IRA		
General	No provision.	Subject to income limits described below, an individual may make a nondeductible contribution (up to $500 annually) to an Education IRA for each child under age 18 and amounts (including earnings) withdrawn for qualified higher education expenses will be tax free and not subject to the 10% early withdrawal penalty. (Effective after 1997.)
Income Limits on Eligibility to Contribute	No provision.	The full $500 contribution is phased out between $150,000 and $160,000 (for married couples) and between $95,000 and $110,000 (for single individuals).
Contributions	No provision.	Contributions must be in cash, made before the beneficiary is 18, and except for rollover contributions must not exceed $500 per year per Education IRA. Contributions are treated as taxable gifts from the IRA contributor to the IRA beneficiary, eligible for the annual gift tax exclusion.
Structural Requirements	No provision.	Like Traditional IRAs, the trustee must be a bank or otherwise IRS-approved trustee, no assets may be invested in life insurance, and assets of two or more Education IRAs may not be comingled except in a common trust fund. The IRA must be designated as an Education IRA when first established.

PROVISION	PRESENT LAW	TAXPAYER RELIEF ACT
Education IRA continued		
Distributions	No provisions.	All qualified distributions are tax free with no early withdrawal penalty. Qualified tax-free distributions are for qualified higher education expenses and may not exceed actual expenses. Qualified higher education expenses include tuition, fees, books, supplies, and equipment required for attendance at eligible higher educational institutions or certain vocational educational schools. Upon death of the beneficiary, all amounts must be distributed to the beneficiary's estate. [All amounts remaining in the IRA must be distributed to the beneficiary when he or she becomes 30 and will be taxable and subject to the early withdrawal penalty—in Committee Report but not statute.]
Designated Beneficiaries	No provision.	Any person under age 18. Change of beneficiary is not a taxable event as along as the change is a family member (ancestor, spouse, child, grandchild, or spouse of child or grandchild).

PROVISION	PRESENT LAW	TAXPAYER RELIEF ACT
Education IRA continued		
Waiver of Early Withdrawal Penalty	No provision.	Distributions that are not for qualified higher education expenses will be taxable and subject to a 10% penalty (similar to Section 72(t) penalty), unless the distribution is on account of the death of the designated beneficiary, the beneficiary's disability, or the distribution is made on account of certain scholarships and allowances.
Rollover Provisions	No provision	Amounts may be rolled over tax free and without the withdrawal penalty from an Education IRA to another Education IRA or the benefit of the same beneficiary or for a member of the family if rolled over within 60 days after distribution. Only one rollover may occur in any 12-month period.
Other Rules	No provisions	Rules concerning payment of IRA on death or divorce, excess contributions, the effect of pledging the account, and the application of the prohibited transaction rules are to be similar to those applicable to Traditional IRAs, except that the payment of qualified higher education expenses will not be subject to the payment of the excise tax on prohibited transactions under Code Section 4975.

EMPLOYEE TAX-DEFERRED PLANS

Some employers sponsor a variety of plans, depending on the company's status. Nonprofit organizations can sponsor 403(b) tax-sheltered annuities. Government agencies can sponsor the 457 programs. And the most common, the 401(k), which allows you to contribute a percentage of your salary up to a certain amount. Like the IRA, these 3 plans allow your contribution to be tax-deductible, whereas the tax on your earnings is deferred until withdrawal. Some 25.2 million Americans took advantage of a 401(k) plan when offered. For some lucky employees, their employers matched the contributions up to a certain percentage or dollar amount as an additional benefit. These matching contributions add additional money in the plan to help an employee build their account faster.

NEW INFORMATION FROM CONGRESS

The U.S. Congress is in the process of approving legislation that would permit Americans to put more money each year into individual retirement accounts and 401(k) plans. The legislation is billed as a way to supplement Social Security and boost the U.S. savings rate from its lowest level in 67 years.

When it passes Congress and becomes law, it would permit workers to make tax-deferred contributions to IRAs of up to $5,000 a year by 2004, rather than the current $2,000. Similar increases would apply for after-tax contributions to Roth IRAs. Maximum contributions to 401(k) plans would rise to $15,000 a year, from $10,500 now, by 2006.

The proposed legislation would not raise income limits that prevent many middle- to upper-income taxpayers from taking advantage of the tax-deferred benefits of IRA contributions. Dissenters also complained that it would not do enough to help low-income workers save more.

The new 529 plan is the latest invention of the IRS to help people save and invest. This national college savings program, author-
ized and created under Section 529 of the Internal Revenue Code
and in partnership with the Ohio Tuition Trust Authority (OTTA),
is to help people save for the costs of higher education. The program
combines tax benefits with professional portfolio management and
allows you to control withdrawals for the life of the account.

SEP Plans

Simplified Employee Pension Plans are similar to IRAs, but are
designed for individuals who are self-employed, and their employees. These plans have been called "Super IRAs." These plans allow
employees to contribute up to 15 percent of their adjusted gross
income. In addition, the contributions are considered a business
expense and lower the owner's base income for tax purposes.
These earnings compound tax-deferred. There are two special benefits of these types of plans. They can be established at the time you
file your taxes, including extensions and there aren't any plan
administration requirements.

Keogh plans are also for self-employed individuals and their
employees, but they have strict administration requirements that
may decrease their advantages.

Own or Loan?

Many African Americans fail to become financially stable
because they don't understand the difference in being an owner,
not a loaner. Most people invest their money in safe investments,
like savings and loans, which in turn pay them the current rate.
Good deal, right? Wrong!

They are normally paid 2–6 percent interest, but their money is
being loaned out at a much higher rate. So those institutions are
making a profit from the use of your money.

Why would someone remain in this position? It's usually because they feel comfortable with the insurance guarantees that require such institutions by law, to insure, up to $100,000 on deposits. But being a loaner can also be considered a barrier to your own financial independence. To get a rate of return that keeps up with inflation, it's a good idea to invest directly in the American economy. This has the potential to really make that investment grow.

THE BOTTOM LINE—INVEST, NOT SAVE

Rather than allowing your savings to be used in this fashion, what can you do to get the rate of return you need to keep ahead? The stock market is a wise place to consider if you want to make meaningful progress toward your financial goals.

Yes, there's always potential loss when investing in stocks, but there is also potential gain. I submit to you, however, that the amount of risk you expose yourself to is offset by the opportunity for a significant return.

If it's a guarantee you're looking for, you must be willing to accept a low return, which has the potential to be even lower because of the effects of inflation. In some cases, it might be good to assume the level of risk in exchange for the potential of significant returns. Only you can decide if you want to be a saver or an investor. The later will take you a long way toward building a secure financial estate.

BENEFITS VERSUS RISKS

What are the risks of participating in the stock market? Everyone has read or heard of stock market "crashes." These crashes, which can happen on any day or within any week, always make the news headlines. These reports tend to scare people away from becoming potential "owners." But any investment deserves to be scrutinized regarding risk. So it doesn't pay to let fear keep you from investigating the potential for significant returns.

An investor who purchases common stock is still better off than one who invested in guaranteed returns. Perhaps you can't afford not to invest based on your goals. Remember the family that invested $1,000 at their child's birth for retirement? Consider what that fund would have looked like today.

By carefully reading the chart below, you'll note the impressive growth over the long haul.

Take a good look at the difference between the investment in stocks and what would have been earned if they had invested in the average fixed-income account. Select a date closest to the year you were born and compare the rates of return on each investment.

TABLE 10.3

Stocks vs. A Fixed Income Investment
$100 per month

Beginning in Year Market**	Cumulative Contribution	Average Fixed Income Account*	Value of Investment in Stock
1930	$76,800	$596,958	$11,875,309
1940	64,800	402,682	4,935,918
1950	52,800	261,774	1,276,508
1960	40,800	152,897	412,612
1970	28,800	75,918	182,268
1980	16,800	28,243	52,719
1990	4,800	5,258	6,172

* With interest compounded annually. Based on historical interest/savings rates supplied by the *Merrill Lynch Ready Assets Trust Rate*. Such deposits offer a guaranteed return of principal and a fixed rate of interest, but no opportunity for capital growth.

** As measured by *Standard and Poor's 500 Index*, an unmanaged index. Past performance is not a guarantee of future results. For illustrative purposes only.

WHAT'S A "BULL" AND "BEAR" MARKET?

You've probably heard the phrase over and over, but what does it mean? These terms signify the cycles of increase or decrease in the stock market as a whole. If it's a "bull market," stocks are rising; conversely, if they are falling, it's termed a "bear market."

Since 1926, the chance of losing money in the stock market over a year's time have only been 30 percent, according to an article in the *Wall Street Journal*. Even though your own gain or loss can be more or less, this form of investment is still the best for long-term goals.

Do You Get the Message?

Due to a variety of circumstances, you may have never thought about events that are thirty or so years into the future. But, hopefully, after reading this chapter, you realize that if you have the desire, discipline, and a little basic knowledge, you can look ahead to security in your retirement years. Answer True or False to each statement.

1. Personal savings and investments are the most common form of retirement savings.

2. The responsibility for planning your retirement is yours.

3. You can rely on the government for your financial security.

4. Your employer is required to plan your retirement.

5. You can plan your retirement only with the help of a financial adviser.

6. Inflation can adversely affect every aspect of your game plan.

7. Tax shelters are only for the rich.

8. IRAs are horrible tax shelters.

9. Security in your retirement years is available if you have the desire, discipline, and a little basic knowledge.

10. Most people are gradually facing the reality that financial self-reliance is a way of life.

Key

1.	T	6.	T
2.	T	7.	F
3.	F	8.	F
4.	F	9.	T
5.	F	10.	T

Chapter 11

MUTUAL FUNDS AND YOUR FUTURE

"Before I ride with a drunk, I'll drive myself."

—STEVIE WONDER
Entertainer

We've already agreed that accumulating income for retirement should be the first priority for all African American families. You've learned the rules of making your money grow. You understand why you should become an owner, not a loaner. Now you need to know the best form of savings or investment, one that will use the advantage of money over time, provide high potential growth, and is a hedge against inflation.

Consider what you already know—traditional savings give low returns and haven't been able to keep pace with inflation. So what's left? The answer is mutual funds. They give you an opportunity to participate in the stock market without having to study and know in detail what stocks to select and how to manage them. And they potentially offer greater returns on your money than most fixed rates vehicles.

Mutual funds have gone from little-known investment choices to the most popular investment vehicles for a lot of African American families.

What Are Mutual Funds?

Mutual funds are investments in the financial markets we've already discussed—stocks, bonds, etc. These funds allow investors to "pool" their money together under the management of an experienced fund manager. This has made them the fastest growing investment vehicle in America.

What does the fund manager do? The manager is a professional in the field who spends time diversifying money into a variety of businesses by purchasing their stocks or bonds. The benefit of having this manager means you can gain from his or her knowledge rather than utilizing your time to understand the market. In addition, you will have investment options that are unavailable to most, whether your temperament and investment objective is aggressive or conservative.

Investors, like you, own shares in the fund according to your investment. You also receive any earnings on that same basis. By law, no more than 5 percent of a fund's assets may be invested in any one security. So, your investment is not considered "high-risk." You can, however, pick your risk because funds are designed to match the "risk-versus-return" preference of every investor. You can monitor your investment in the daily paper. And you automatically receive annual statements showing your income and capital gains and when you made a transaction.

Equity funds are the most aggressive because their investors can endure a higher risk for the potential of a higher return. Balanced funds are for the average investor who wants to combine equity and income investments. Income funds are for investors who want current income with moderate risk.

Mutual funds are very popular among African Americans because they are a simple, convenient, and inexpensive means to invest in a portfolio of securities. Rather than tying up your money for years to get the maximum rate of return, you get potential growth, in addition to access to your money if you decide to sell your shares. According to law, once you sell your shares, mutual-fund administrators are required to mail your redemption check within seven days of the initial request.

Did you know mutual funds give you the opportunity to make money three different ways? Dividends are paid on earnings of the fund, capital gains are distributed, and the shares held appreciate. Mutual funds are convenient because you can invest in a number of ways, based on what suits your individual needs. You can use any of the following investment strategies:

1. **A lump-sum investment.** If you are lucky enough to get a "windfall," you can invest it and get a head start on your investment goals.

2. **A voluntary investment.** If you periodically find extra money to invest, you may contribute to the fund at any time. Because this deals with extra funds, you would not want to depend on this method of reaching your investment goal.

3. **A systematic investment.** You can use discipline and commit yourself to investing a certain amount each payday or on a monthly basis. This is the most sure and sound way to accumulate those assets you need to meet your goal.

THE "BEAR" ADVANTAGE

Everyone is aware of the advantage of systematic savings. The same applies to investing in the stock market. Even though you shouldn't invest according to what's happening in the market, you should still systematically invest to make your money grow. When you do this, you can actually take advantage of market fluctuations and acquire more shares.

Since your money isn't locked in, you control when and if you want to make withdrawals, in addition to how much. If you decide to take your money, there are many options available with a mutual fund. You can:

1. Redeem your shares at net asset value.
2. Take out dividends and declare capital gains.
3. Take out any portion at any time and let the balance grow.

INVESTMENT TIPS—MUTUAL FUNDS AT THEIR BEST

1. This is a great long-term vehicle. Over time, stocks outperform any other type of investments.
2. Make investing a systematic habit. Most experts don't try to anticipate the market; why should you?
3. Remember our lessons from compounding interest. Re-invest your dividends so you can build financial security quicker.
4. Consider your age. While you're young, you can invest more aggressively. If retirement is near, chose a conservative fund.

BE CREATIVE—COMBINE MUTUAL FUNDS AND IRAs

We've discussed the wisdom of contributing to an IRA and you understand the benefit of investing in a mutual fund. Why not have a mutual fund within your IRA?

Let's Take a Look at the Growth Figures

- In 1998, with the advent of the new Roth IRAs, the total number of IRA accounts rose almost 20 percent.
- By the end of 1993, IRAs accounted for 23 percent of mutual-fund assets (excluding annuities).
- In 1992, IRA accounts were 30.7 percent of all mutual-fund accounts.
- In 1993, mutual fund IRA assets grew over 35 percent of 1992. In 1992, mutual fund IRA assets grew over 25 percent of 1991. In 1991, mutual fund IRA assets grew over 33 percent of 1990.

OUR FINAL OPTION: VARIABLE ANNUITIES

Once you've maximized your IRA and other retirement options, variable annuities are yet another option to be considered. They have many of the same rules that govern other retirement accounts, such as withdrawal age. And when you reach retirement, you can begin withdrawing. Variable annuities allow you to select from a variety of funds with different investment objectives, similar to mutual funds. They are best used as advantages for tax investment after you've used other options.

SOME FINAL PROS AND CONS

Risk and reward always go hand in hand. The greater the risk, the greater the potential for reward. This is also true of stock mutual funds.

Equity investment shows a trend of consistent growth, compared to a comparable investment in a savings account. Comparing the $10,000 stock mutual fund investment made on January 1, 1990, and held until December 31, 2000, to a similar investment in a savings account, the stock would have tripled to more than $33,000 at an assumed rate of 12.5 percent.

Even though there are no guarantees, stock mutual funds seem to offer better opportunities to increase your initial investment.

READING THE FINANCIAL PAGES: A FINANCIAL SCOREBOARD

How many times have you seen someone reading the financial pages and wondered what it all means? The financial pages can be thought of as the "box scores," much like the sports pages. They report current prices on many types of investments, like stocks, bonds, and mutual funds. They also report current interest rates, economic trends, and business activities.

Stock market—report of the bulls and bears. The *Dow Jones Industrial Average* is the most widely read record of market activity. It gives you a brief composite of thirty key manufacturing and service markets. *Standard & Poor's 500* is a much broader index. Most investors read these reports as a basis to evaluate daily activity, in addition to measuring the fluctuation of individual stocks.

Daily stock listings. These listings supply data for the investor to work with, but they are for anyone who wants to follow the increase or decrease of the price of stocks for specific companies. The daily listings look like this:

TABLE 11.1
Stock Market Listings

1/2	3	4/5	6	7	8	9	10	11
52 Week High/low	Stock Name	Div%/ Yield	PE Ratio	Sales 100s	High	Low	Last	Change
48/33	XYZ Co.	1.4/0.48	24	563	38	33	35	4

Each column provides key information on the stock. The first two columns, respectively, tell you how the stock has performed, the highest and lowest price the stock has achieved over the previous fifty-two weeks. Column three lists the name of the stock. In columns four and five, "dividend" reports the company's declared divided, and "yield" tells you the percentage of return that dividend achieved.

Column six, "PE Ratio," is a little more complex. This is the key investment indicator of stock value. It's sometimes called the "multiplier" because it's achieved by dividing the price of the stock dividends by the company's annual earnings per share.

Column seven lists the sales volume in hundreds of shares for the previous day, thus Sales 100s. The figure listed in the chart is 563, meaning 56,300 shares were sold.

The next three columns are self-explanatory. They list the previous day's stock prices. High means the highest price that day, low means the lowest price and final is the stock's price at the day's end.

Column eleven tells how much, in fractions of a dollar, a share of that stock changed from the previous day.

Bond tables. Bonds are not recorded on the financial pages of most daily newspapers. They are traded "over the counter," which means they are sold without the assistance of a broker.

Mutual fund listings are easier to read than stock and bond tables.

TABLE 11.2
Mutual Fund Listings

1	2	3	4
Name of Fund	Sell	Buy	Change
Voy	17.68	17.63	-.05

Column one lists the name of the fund, column two lists the price a seller would have paid for one share at the close of business the previous day. Column three is the price a buyer would have received for one share at the close of business the previous day. And column four tells how much, in fractions of a dollar, a share changed from the previous day.

Once you buy your first share of stock or watch your mutual-fund investment, reading the financial pages will take on a new meaning.

Do You Get the Message?

Now you should know the best form of savings or investment. For the average African American family, it's better to use methods that will use the advantage of money over time, provide high potential growth, and be a hedge against inflation. Your understanding of this is essential to your financial success. Test your self by answering True or False to each statement.

1. Traditional savings give low returns and haven't been able to keep pace with inflation.

2. Mutual funds are investments in the financial markets, stocks, bonds, etc. that allow investors to pool their money together under the management of an experienced fund manager.

3. Mutual funds allow you to make money three different ways—through dividends, capital gains, and appreciated shares.

4. Inflation, debt financing, and earned-income tax credits are ways that mutual funds allow you to make money.

5. With mutual funds you can make withdrawals at your own discretion.

6. Trying to anticipate the market instead of systematic investing is the best way to get high returns.

7. Accumulating income for retirement should be the first priority for all African American families.

8. Mutual funds potentially offer greater returns on your money than most fixed rates vehicles.

9. Mutual funds have become the most popular investment vehicles for a lot of African American families.

10. Mutual funds give you an opportunity to participate in the stock market without having to study and know in detail what stocks to select and how to manage them.

Key

1. T		6. F	
2. T		7. T	
3. T		8. T	
4. F		9. T	
5. T		10. T	

Chapter 12

INSURANCE: WHY YOU NEED IT AND HOW TO CHOOSE IT

"Honey, eighty percent of the people could care less about your problems, and the other twenty percent are glad that you have them."

—JACKIE "MOMS" MABLEY
Comedienne

Have you ever experienced a fire in your home, a burglary or automobile accident? If your answer is yes, you know how these incidents can change your financial picture in a few minutes. What takes years to accumulate, can be lost in a matter of moments. The potential for these losses make insurance a necessity. There are many options available based on your need and desire for protection. Let's take a look at homeowners insurance first.

PROTECTING YOUR HOME

This type of insurance covers different types of disasters that could damage your home or belongings. Most policies protect three major areas:

- the dwelling
- the contents
- liability

Make sure to give your agent a good idea of what's important to you so you can determine the best policy for your circumstances. Here are a few different types of coverage you need to consider:

Law or ordinance.

This type of coverage ensures that you will be able to rebuild your house at higher building standards. A basic policy is considered the bare necessity and doesn't mean your problem is solved if you make a claim. Many times a loss occurs at a time when rebuilding involves new, higher building-code standards or construction material, which will likely cost more than if you were only restoring to original standards.

Inflation Guard.

What would it cost for you to rebuild your home? This needs to be considered whenever you buy homeowners insurance. Costs are continually rising, and you must make sure your coverage keeps pace with inflation. Utilize the experience of your agent to help you determine how much is enough.

Additional Structures.

All detached structures should be included in your basic plan. A guest house, workshop, studio, swimming pool, carport, etc. are considered additional structures. Normally these additions are automatically covered for a maximum of 10 percent of the value of the home.

Replacement Cost.

Whether it's a home or apartment, you need to find out what possessions are protected in your basic policy. Usually plans provide only for replacement according to the depreciated value. But when you are replacing your valuables, it's unlikely you would replace them with old ones.

Personal Articles.

You may want to supplement your coverage for items that are worth more than the special sublimits. Chances are the more personal the article, the most devastated you would be if it was stolen.

Loss Assessment.

Living in a condominium presents a different set of issues. Even though you would have a basic policy, it's possible for your condominium association to file a claim for a loss that exceeds its own coverage. As a member of the association, you would be asked to make up the cost difference.

INSURANCE TIPS FOR HOMEOWNERS

- On average, most of these policies provide only a cash settlement when the damaged item is replaced. If it isn't replaced, you will receive only the depreciated or "actual cash" value.
- Protect your family's dream home by insuring it for real replacement cost, not the current market value. Always take into consideration how much it might cost to rebuild your home from scratch. Consider each upgrade, and amend your policy as necessary.

- Supplements for personal articles or "floaters" can be expensive, so make sure you are willing to cover a big financial loss rather than a sentimental one.
- Keep a visual record of your belongings along with receipts of sale. Keep this record in another location outside your home.

IN SOME STATES IT'S THE LAW: AUTO INSURANCE

In some states, automobile owners are required to buy minimum coverage to pay medical expenses for injuries sustained in an auto accident, regardless of who's at fault. This is known as "no-fault" insurance. States that require this type of insurance will not allow the driver who is at fault to be sued for an accident unless the medical expenses are over a certain limit, prescribed by the state.

In other states, you may still be required to buy insurance, but you have the right to sue drivers who've caused you injury, regardless of how high the dollar amount of your medical bills. These states don't have "no-fault" insurance.

In any case, you have to stay abreast of new rulings because states often change their laws. In addition, these changes sometimes are opportunities to save money. There are a few important ways to save on your premiums.

First, consider paying a higher deductible. A standard level for comprehensive deductibles is $250, whereas an additional $500 is recommended for collision. A savings of 15–20 percent could result if you have both deductibles. You could have lower deductibles, such as $100/$250, but it would cost more in the long run.

Justifying a lower deductible would mean the driver would need to have more than twice as many losses as the average driver. Traditionally, the submission of claims less than $1,000 causes premiums to rise. As a consequence, many people never submit them.

Finally, it pays to be a good driver. Obeying the law is a good way to save money. Speeding, drunken driving, or disregarding traffic signs are all good examples of circumstances that can cause your driving record to be compromised by moving violations, thus driving up your insurance premiums.

TABLE 12.1

How a Driving Record Affects Premiums

Type of Policy	One Ticket Can Raise Rates By:	One DUI or Three Speeding Tickets Can Raise Rates By:
Single Car Policy	40%	150%
Multiple Car Policy	20%	75%

Source: Typical Travelers 1994 rating plans, may vary by state.

THE COST OF COVERAGE

Besides the community that you reside in, there are three primary factors that determine how much you will pay for automobile insurance: your age, driving record, and the type of vehicle you drive. A luxury or sports car is going to cost you a lot more than a family vehicle.

You may already have some coverage or services from other sources, such as your medical-insurance plan or auto-service-club membership. It pays to know what you have so duplication and waste won't happen. If your automobile falls into the following two categories, you are sure to pay more for your insurance:

- If you own a sports car, specialty car or small to mid-sized imported car you should be prepared to pay more to insure, repair, and maintain them.
- If you own a high performance car with a powerful engine your rates will be high.

Conversely, the following seven points are examples of ways to save money on your automobile insurance:

- Make sure your automobile has air bags, antitheft devices and antilock breaks. These are safety features that could qualify you for additional discounts.
- Because they are larger, four-door sedans are the safest cars and typically cost less to insure.
- It will save money if you can purchase your auto and home-owners insurance from the same company.
- Senior citizens fifty-five years and older may be eligible for discounts.
- Becoming part of a carpool may qualify you for lower rates.
- If your teenagers get good grades in driver's education, they may be eligible for a break.
- If you take an approved defensive driving course, you could qualify for a discount, depending on the state of your residence.

Take a look at the following chart listing types of coverage. It may help you make the best decision for your circumstances.

TABLE 12.2 Insurance Coverage Options

Type of Coverage	Description	Tips
Bodily Injury Liability	**Bodily Injury Liability** covers injuries that happen to passengers in your car or other cars or to pedestrians when you are responsible for causing the accident. It also may cover both you and your family members when driving someone else's car with permission.	**Tip:** The more assets you have, the more coverage you need to protect yourself from lawsuits. Most states have a minimum required coverage limit of $20,000, but you can usually purchase up to $500,000.
Property Damage Liability	**Property Damage Liability** covers you for damages to another person's property, such as another person's car or possessions that were harmed by your car.	**Tip:** Losses are usually lower than those for Bodily Injury. However, keep in mind that there are many expensive luxury cars on the road worth more than $30,000.
Uninsured Motorists	**Uninsured Motorists** covers you and your family if you are injured in an accident that was caused by someone else *not* covered by auto insurance, including a hit-and-run driver. In most states, it also covers you if the driver at fault has auto insurance but not enough to cover all your damages.	**Tip:** Relatively inexpensive coverage, so you may want to buy limits that are equal to your Bodily Injury limits.
Medical Payments	**Medical Payments** covers you and your family for injuries sustained in an auto accident, regardless of who is at fault. Some states require this coverage.	**Tip:** Most comprehensive health insurance covers the same expenses. Buy enough Medical Payments coverage to cover the deductibles, co-payments and other out-of-pocket costs from your health insurance. Also, if someone in your household does not have health insurance, you should buy as much as you can afford.

Type of Coverage	Description	Tips
Collision	**Collision** covers the cost of repairing or replacing your car after an accident, regardless of who is at fault.	**Tip:** If your car is more than seven years old, you might decide the cost of coverage just isn't worth the price. If you drop this type of coverage, you'll pay for repairs out of your own pocket when and if they are needed. **Rule of Thumb:** Buy Collision if the annual premium is less than 10% of the car's current value, minus the deductible.
Comprehensive	**Comprehensive** protects your car, not your family. It covers damages for most circumstances other than collision, including theft, fire, vandalism, hail, and animal contact.	**Tip:** Just like Collision, it sometimes makes sense to self-insure if you drive an older car that's paid for. **Rule of Thumb:** Buy Comprehensive if the annual premium is less than 10% of the car's current value, minus the deductible.
Towing		**Tip:** Don't purchase this if you are enrolled in an auto club that provides emergency road service. You are duplicating coverage needlessly.
Rental Reimbursement		**Tip:** If you can do without one of your cars for any length of time, you probably don't need this type of coverage.

Did You Get the Message?

Everything we own can be lost in a matter of moments in a fire, a burglary or automobile accident, changing our financial picture in a few minutes. Unfortunately, many of us fail to protect our assets because we are either underinsured or not insured at all. Hopefully, you are ready to explore the many options available to you and prepared to take action to acquire or maintain the appropriate coverages. Answer True or False to each statement.

1. When selecting an insurance policy, you should tell you agent what's important to you so you can determine the best policy for your circumstances.

2. Inflation guard, replacement costs, and loss assessment are three examples of investment strategies.

3. Two types of insurance coverage are mutual funds and stock options.

4. There are three primary factors that determine how much you pay for car insurance: your age, driving record, and the type of vehicle.

5. Lifestyle, television-viewing habits, and professional degrees are relevant when considering the amount of insurance coverage that you are required to get.

6. Some states require that you have automobile insurance.

7. It is best to insure your family's dream home by having an iron fence placed around you home and getting a dog.

8. It is best to insure your family's dream home by insuring it for real replacement cost, not the current market value.

9. It is best to insure your family's dream home by insuring it for the current market value only.

10. Usually plans provide only for re placement according to the depreciated value.

Key

1.	T	6.	T
2.	T	7.	F
3.	F	8.	T
4.	T	9.	F
5.	F	10.	T

Chapter 13

PROTECT YOURSELF: GUARD YOUR FINANCIAL FUTURE

"The best preparation for tomorrow is to do your best today."

—ANONYMOUS

Very few people are overinsured. In 2001, the face amount of the average individual life insurance policy in America was $18,220. If death happened to the breadwinner, how many years would that amount provide for a family's current lifestyle? After those years had passed, how would they live?

The average death claim paid in that same year was $11,737 per policy. This figure is startlingly lower among African Americans. And it is certainly not commensurate with the average cost of living for a family of four. These statistics point out two startling realizations: The average African American individual has not prepared the family for the inevitable—death, and survivors try to continue to live in the style to which they are accustomed. Since having adequate life insurance protection is important, it's crucial that you get the best value possible.

NEVER BOUGHT, ALWAYS SOLD—LIFE INSURANCE

Life insurance is a basic element in your financial plan. No one wants to consider death, but you know it's a fact that you will die someday. People tend to avoid the subject of death because it is unpleasant and, they likewise avoid buying life insurance. A lot of African Americans buy it from someone who asks, without doing research or being sure of what they've purchased.

FACTS OF LIFE

Life insurance is not that complicated, and it really doesn't insure your life. It insures your income, so to speak, so when you die, your family will be protected against a loss of your income. It's the earning potential life insurance is meant to protect. Anyone with financial obligations needs life insurance.

If you have a nonworking spouse and/or children, your need for life insurance is greater. Conversely, if your spouse doesn't work, he or she also needs to be insured by taking into consideration what it would cost to replace all the roles that individual plays. How much would it cost to replace a full-time cook, chauffeur, maid, dog sitter, and someone to literally pay the bills for the next 30 years? When thought of in this manner, insurance is bought to ensure a standard of living and peace of mind.

Too little life insurance would leave your family vulnerable after your death because they might have to tap into other financial sources for supplemental income. This would destroy the long-term goals and dreams your family planned so hard to realize, like that college education for each of your children.

WHOLE-LIFE INSURANCE

Whole-life, or cash-value insurance, is sometimes known as permanent insurance. It is based on the belief that you will need insurance coverage throughout your entire life. It has a cash value and two additional benefits. The first benefit is the insurance policy, and the second benefit is some form of savings or investment feature. Since these features cannot be purchased separately, the cost of whole-life insurance is higher than term insurance, which we will discuss in more detail shortly. This feature is known as "bundling."

With whole-life policies, the cash accumulation can be withdrawn and then invested, but using one option affects the other. Take a look at the following profile comparison to understand the difference.

TABLE 13.1
Profile: Healthy male, age 35, preferred nonsmoker $200,000 coverage

Insurance Type	Annual Cost
Whole Life	$3,208
Term Life	$ 307

Premium based on the average participating whole-life premium and annual renewable term premium of leading whole-life and term plans of five of the largest insurance companies. *1994 Best's Flitcraft Compend.*

TERM INSURANCE—A BETTER FIT FOR YOUR FAMILY?

Term insurance offers pure death protection and no financial incentives, as whole-life insurance can. Having the right insurance protection for your family's financial life cycle can make a major difference in your cash flow. Simply put, if you die during your "term," prechosen by you, your beneficiaries collect the death benefit prescribed in the policy.

When your family is young, you can easily purchase enough low-cost term insurance to protect against the loss of your earning power. Typically, it's less expensive than whole-life insurance and allows you to purchase maximum protection with minimum funds. Taking into consideration your responsibilities at this time in your life, this is when you need insurance the most.

There are a few different types of term insurance. Annual renewable term insurance is purchased for a one-year period at a specific price. When the year is completed, you can reapply, but it will be at a higher rate because you will be a year older. It's affordable when you are younger but becomes more expensive the longer you live.

Level term insurance is purchased for a longer, specified period, usually 10–20 years. During this term, the premium stays level. It averages the cost of insurance over the entire period.

Modified level term insurance has a higher first-year premium but is dramatically reduced during the remainder of the policy. The benefit of having such a policy is that once the initial payment is completed, the subsequent cost is much less.

Decreasing term insurance allows you to pay a level premium throughout the term of the policy, but as you age, the face amount of coverage decreases. The "Theory of Decreasing Responsibility" is the basis for this insurance and makes more sense when you consider age and accountability.

WHAT'S ENOUGH?—A COMMON INSURANCE QUESTION

When considering enough insurance protection, a good rule of thumb is five to ten times your annual salary, taking into account your cash assets, dependents, and lifestyle. Some guides consider $100,000 coverage on the breadwinner and riders of $50,000 on each child to be the standard. No matter what coverage you decide is adequate, having only one policy will mean no separate fees, more cost you can do without.

Also, you need to remember that purchasing insurance is like buying any other product: You need to get the most for your money. Your goal for adequate protection should always take cost into account. Simply remember to evaluate your insurance needs periodically, because there may be a better value at a lower cost. It's also wise to avoid extra options that will increase the cost. One exception would be a waiver of premium benefit. This provides for payment of your premium if you become disabled and unable to maintain payment. Even though situations differ, here are some guidelines that can provide direction:

Replace a policy when:

- The policy is old and possibly outdated.
- Other vehicles could better meet your investment needs.
- You have several policies that could be combined for a lower rate.

Be careful about replacing a policy:

- When you are in poor health or uninsurable.
- When you have a good, comprehensive competitive policy. Don't give up a good value for what appears to a better one.
- When you've had the policy for many years. You will lose benefits if you replace it.
- There are no rules of thumb. Replacement is an individual matter taking your age, special needs, and income level into account.
- Always ask for a policy illustration and examine your options.

Other points to consider:

- Any financial purchase could have estate tax consequences if you are wealthy. Be careful when making insurance purchases or replacements.
- There is a two-year window of opportunity for most policies to be contested. Consider this when thinking of a purchase. Be aware, though, that in some states insurance companies waive the contestability requirement if the policy is a replacement.

ESTATE AND ESTATE TAXES

The Tax Act of 1997

This tax act increased the present unified credit and increased the exemptions from $600,000 in 1997 to $1,000,000 in 2006. The chart below gives the yearly exemption amounts:

TABLE 13.2
Tax Act in Annual Increases

YEAR	EXEMPTION AMOUNT
1998	$ 625,000
1999	$ 650,000
2000	$ 675,000
2001	$ 675,000
2002	$ 700,000
2003	$ 700,000
2004	$ 850,000
2005	$ 950,000
2006 and thereafter	$ 1,000,000

Life insurance is another way to provide the cash necessary to pay estate taxes when they become due. It can also be a way of avoiding delays when a will is in probate. Nevertheless, when you've built an estate large enough to be subject to taxes, you will need expert advice to make sure you're not paying more than necessary.

The Tax Act of 1997 also excludes a "family-owned business interest" from the estate as long as the interest does not exceed $1.3 million. Looking at the chart, in 1998 a family business exemption could well be $600,000.

To qualify for the family business exemption, a decedent must have materially participated in the business for at least five of eight years preceding the death of the owner. In addition, the business passing to qualified heirs must exceed 50 percent of the decedent's estate, while no more than 35 percent of the business's gross income may be personal holding company income. To the extent the business holds excess cash or marketable securities, the value of a qualifying business interest is reduced.

This tax code has complicated provisions, and you should consult your tax adviser before making any decisions that could impact your estate.

Do You Get the Message?

The average paid death claim is startlingly low among African Americans. It is certainly not commensurate with the average cost of living for a family of four, making it a startling realization that we have not prepared the family for the inevitable. You should now understand how to get adequate life-insurance protection and the best value possible. What do you think? Answer True or False to each statement.

1. Life insurance doesn't insure your life, it insures your income.

2. Replace a policy when other vehicles could better meet your investment needs.

3. Wealthy people don't have to worry about estate tax consequences.

4. When considering enough insurance protection, a good rule of thumb is five to ten times your annual salary.

5. Whole-life insurance offers no financial incentives.

6. A lot of African Americans buy life insurance from someone who asks, without doing research or being sure of what they've purchased.

7. Life insurance is not a basic element in your financial plan.

8. If you have a nonworking spouse and/or children, your need for life insurance is less.

9. Insurance should be bought to ensure a standard of living and peace of mind.

10. Too little life insurance would leave your family vulnerable after your death.

Key

1.	T	6.	T
2.	T	7.	F
3.	F	8.	F
4.	T	9.	T
5.	F	10.	T

Chapter 14

NEW INCOME TAX RATES HELP YOU SAVE MONEY

"Helped are those who create anything at all, for they shall relive the thrill of their own conception...."

—ALICE WALKER

African Americans began getting checks in the mail in the summer 2001 of up to $300 for individuals, $500 for single parents and $600 for couples. This reflected the first year of a new 10 percent income tax rate on the initial $6,000 of an individual's income, $12,000 for married couples.

Most other income tax rates changed as well. By 2006, the old 39.6 percent rate is expected to fall to 35 percent.

In addition:

- The standard deduction for married couples will gradually grow beginning in 2005 so that it becomes twice that of single taxpayers. The 15 percent tax bracket will also be gradually adjusted beginning in 2005 to cover more of married couples' incomes until it doubles that of singles.
- The $500 tax credit for children will rise to $600 in 2001 and $1,000 by 2010.
- The inheritance tax would be repealed by 2010. Exempted estates would gradually rise from $675,000 now to $3.5 million.
- Contribution limits for IRAs and 401(k)-type plans will expand. From $2,000 for IRA's to $5,000 and even more for 401(k) type plans $10,500 to $15,000.

How To Get Going

Start saving early: When today's newborn starts college in 2019, it likely will cost $136,217 to send him or her to a public college and $295,321 to private school, according to the College Board. In an ideal world, parents should put aside $225 to $488 per month from the time the child is born to have enough to manage all expenses. This is not an ideal world, not for us.

Live on less: Take a hard look at your spending money and cut back wherever you can on extras so you can learn to live on less than your salary. Most people spend 70 percent to 80 percent of their incomes on fixed and flexible expenses and have no idea where the rest of the money goes. Make a budget and stick to it.

Use automatic investment options: Set aside whatever money you can in a fund that allows automatic electronic transfer of money. When the funds are automatically deducted from your paycheck, saving becomes forced.

Re-evaluate savings: As children enter grade school, families should evaluate savings and meet with a financial planner. It might be more realistic to save less when a child is a baby and more when they reach junior high school.

Try to catch up: If one parent stayed home while the children were young, the couple might be able to catch up financially if that parent starts working again when children are in school. Families can try to save half of the second income to help pay for college. Bonuses and tax refunds can be invested. Involve teens in saving: If you inherit money, you can take advantage of the new 529 Savings Plan. Up to $50,000 per parent can be invested as a lump sum in the child's name without triggering a gift tax. The money grows tax deferred and is taxed at the child's rate when withdrawn. At that point, only the financial gains are taxed.

Under current law there are five income tax rates, and if current law goes unchanged for the next five years, a married couple filing jointly will be facing the following rates and brackets in 2006:

- a 15 percent tax on their first $51,350 in taxable income
- 28 percent on income between $51,350 and $124,050
- 31 percent between $124,050 and $189,050
- 36 percent between $189,050 and $337,650; and
- 39.6 percent on all taxable income over $337,650.

Under President Bush's plan, tax rates would gradually fall between 2002 and 2006 (see Table 14.1). In 2006 the changes would be fully phased in, and there would be four rates. A married couple filing jointly would then pay:

- a 10 percent tax on their first $12,000 of taxable income
- 15 percent on income between $12,000 and $51,350
- 25 percent between $51,350 and $189,050, and
- 33 percent on all taxable income over $189,050.

All of these changes to the rates would be implemented gradually over five years.

TABLE 14.1

How the Bush Plan Would Implement
New Individual Income Tax Rates

2001 (current law)	2002	2003	2004	2005	2006
39.6%	38%	37%	36%	35%	33%
36%	35%	35%	34%	34%	
31%	30%	29%	28%	27%	25%
28%	27%	27%	26%	26%	
15%	15%	15%	15%	15%	15%
	14%	13%	12%	11%	10%

Source: Joint Committee on Taxation

Under current law, filers receive a $500 tax credit for each dependent child under 17 years of age. The benefits of this credit are gradually phased out, however, for single filers with adjusted gross incomes over $75,000 and joint filers with AGIs over $110,000.

Under President Bush's plan:

• The per-child tax credit would double from $500 to $1,000, and the point at which the taxpayer starts to lose the benefit of the credit would rise to $200,000 for both single and joint filers.

Both of these changes would be implemented gradually over five years. The child credit would be $600 in 2002, $700 in 2003, $800 in 2004, $900 in 2005, and $1,000 in 2006. Similarly, the income level at which a single taxpayer starts to lose the benefit of the credit would rise $25,000 each year until it reaches $200,000: from $75,000 (current law) to $100,000 in 2002, $125,000 in 2003, $150,000 in 2004, $175,000 in 2005, and finally to $200,000 in 2006. Couples filing joint tax returns currently start to lose the benefit of the credit at $110, 000. That would rise in $18,000 increments annually, to $128,000 in 2002, to $146,000 in 2003, to $164,000 in 2004, to $182,000 in 2005, and finally to $200,000 in 2006.

- Taxpayers could contribute up to $5,000 per child each year to an educational savings account. These funds could be used to defray elementary, secondary, and collegiate educational expenses.

Under current law, two-income married couples with similar incomes often pay higher income taxes than they would if they were unmarried, filing single tax returns. To partially alleviate this so-called marriage penalty, the Bush plan would:

- Grant up to a $3,000 deduction to two-earner families whose tax returns are married filing jointly; and
- Raise the income cutoff on single taxpayers' eligibility for the per child credit from $75,000 to $200,000; and raise it for married couples from $110,000 to $200,000.

CREATED BY PROGRESSIVE RATES AND POPULAR DEDUCTIONS, MARRIAGE PENALTY IS DECRIED BY BOTH PARTIES

Looking for a way to avoid the marriage penalty? Here's a simple way: Just marry someone whose income is much higher or much lower than yours is. Do that and you may even receive a marriage bonus. That's the flip side of the "marriage penalty" —a side that many people are unaware of. Recent passage of H.R. 4810, the Marriage Tax Relief Reconciliation Act of 2000, by both houses of Congress has increased awareness of the marriage penalty and bonus by once again bringing this complex issue into the spotlight.

The bill was approved in July by the House (271 to 156) and

Senate (60 to 34). On August 6, President Clinton vetoed the bill as he had promised he would, and on September 13 the House failed to override the veto. The vote was 270 in favor of the override, including 49 Democrats, against 158 votes to sustain the veto. President Bush's proposed tax plan takes a simpler approach to relieving the marriage penalty than last year's legislation (see Table 14.2).

A marriage penalty occurs when the tax liability of a married couple filing jointly is greater than the sum of the filers' liabilities would be if they were single. This is not as simple as it sounds; it is not an actual additional tax levied on all married couples filing jointly. Rather, it is the result of the complex interactions of the more than sixty provisions of the tax code that vary with marital status, most of which have the potential to confer penalties or bonuses.

The two provisions most often responsible are the standard deduction and the differing widths of tax brackets for single and married filers, although many other provisions can have an effect, including the Earned Income Tax Credit (EITC), limitations on capital losses, home mortgage interest deductions, and education credits. The size of a penalty or bonus is determined by the couple's income, the way the income is split between the two, the number of dependents and the amount of itemized and standard deductions.

The Congressional Budget Office (CBO) estimates that in 1996, 42 percent of married couples incurred penalties, with the average penalty totaling $1,380, and 51 percent of couples received bonuses averaging $1,300 per couple. In 1999, 48 percent are estimated to have incurred penalties and 41 percent received bonuses.

Paul and Lisa Meet the Marriage Penalty

Table 14.3 illustrates a marriage penalty incurred by two people who each earn $40,000. There are two reasons for their $1,490 penalty.

First, the standard deduction for joint filers is not twice that of a single filer. This means that two unmarried taxpayers together have a standard deduction larger than the one they would have as a couple. Now that Paul and Lisa are married, they lose $1,400 of the combined standard deductions they had as single filers. The result is an increase in their taxable income: As single filers they would have a combined taxable income of $65,900, while that amount more than doubles when they file jointly.

Second, as a couple, Paul and Lisa have a larger percentage of their taxable income taxed at a higher rate. This is because the breakpoint for moving from the 15 percent tax bracket to the 28 percent bracket is $25,750 for single filers and $43,050 for couples filing jointly. Since the joint filer tax brackets are not twice as wide as the brackets for singles, often the part of a couple's income that falls into the higher bracket is greater than the total that would fall into that bracket if both people filed singly. Sometimes part of a couple's income is pushed into a bracket that is higher than the bracket either person would fall into singly.

In this example, Paul and Lisa would each have 22 percent of their taxable income taxed at 28 percent; jointly, they have 36 percent of their taxable income taxed at 28 percent. Due to the combination of the joint filer standard deduction and joint filer brackets, they have over a quarter of their gross income taxed at 28 percent; if they filed separately, it would be only 18 percent.

Paul and Lisa can blame a woman named Vivien Kellerns for their marriage penalty. Kellerns was a single businesswoman who founded War Widows of America. Members were either widows or, like Kellerns, single women who claimed they had never married because WWII had created a shortage of single men.

In the 1960s Kellerns and her group protested what they considered to be a singles penalty: At the time, two single people often paid more than a married couple with the same income, sometimes as much as 40 percent more. The higher tax on singles resulted from Congress's 1948 joint-return provisions, which allowed married couples to file jointly and pay double the single-filer tax on one half of their combined taxable income. The joint-filer provisions negated the effect of some states' community property laws, which had been passed in an attempt to lower the federal tax burdens of those states' residents. The joint-filer provisions also ensured that all couples with the same income were taxed equally, regardless of whether one or both spouses had an income.

In 1969, after much media attention and many tea bags mailed to members of Congress (a reminder of the Boston Tea Party), Vivien Kellerns and her allies achieved victory: Congress passed legislation that resulted in a "marriage penalty" for some couples— mainly upper-middle-income couples at first—while creating a bonus for others. Subsequent legislation increased the number of couples who received a penalty.

VACATIONING SINGLE

For a real-life example of a marriage penalty, consider the case of a Maryland couple, David and Angela Boyter, who generated national publicity and media attention (as well as some negative attention from the IRS) in the 1970s by marrying and divorcing three times in order to avoid the marriage penalty. After each divorce they used the money they saved in taxes to pay for a Caribbean vacation. After the third divorce they announced plans to remain together but unmarried until the marriage penalty was eliminated.

MARY AND BOB GET A BONUS

In our fictional example, Paul and Lisa are typical of a couple incurring a penalty in that they both earn the same amount. Couples in which one person earns much less than the other or has no income at all tend to receive bonuses, while couples where both people earn roughly the same amount tend to receive penalties. In general, an income split greater than 70/30 is likely to lead to a bonus.

In the second example (Table 14.3) a couple with a large disparity in income level receives a bonus. Mary is a newly minted attorney earning $80,000 and her husband, Bob, is currently unemployed and has no income.

Three factors are responsible for their $4,146 bonus.

First, the standard deduction, which penalized the first couple, works in Bob and Mary's favor. By herself, Mary could claim a standard deduction of $4,300, while Bob could claim none since he has no income. Filing jointly, they can claim a deduction of $7,200–$2,900 greater than the deduction Mary would receive alone. This deduction saves them $899 ($2,900 taxed at the 31 percent marginal rate that Mary would be subject to by herself).

Bracket size also works in this couple's favor. Although not twice as large as those for single filers, joint filers' brackets are still large enough to create bonuses for some couples. As a single filer, Mary would have $10,500 of her income taxed at 31 percent; when she files jointly, the wider brackets keep all of her income at the 15 and 28 percent rates, thus saving the couple $2,395.

Finally, if Bob were single he could not use his personal exemption, since he has no income. Filing jointly, he can use the exemption, which, when combined with Mary's, saves the couple $853 ($2,750 taxed at 31 percent).

A Tax Foundation Special Report published in 1998 about the marriage penalty explains that the three fundamental pillars of the current tax system affecting joint filers are contradictory, so that tinkering with the current code can never satisfy both single and married taxpayers. The three principles are a progressive rate structure, neutrality with regard to marriage (two single filers who together earn the same amount as a married couple should face the same tax liability as the married couple), and equal treatment of couples (two couples with the same income should pay the same amount of tax, regardless of each couple's income split). The current tax system satisfies only the first of these principles, and without fundamental tax reform, all three can never be satisfied.

The CBO recognizes six major types of provisions that have been proposed as solutions to the marriage penalty: widening the tax brackets and raising the standard deduction for joint filers; exempting some of the lower-earning spouse's income from taxation; expanding the parameters of the EITC; allowing couples to choose the filing status that results in the lower tax burden; some sort of fundamental tax reform, such as a consumption tax or flat tax; and requiring spouses to file individual tax returns.

The only change that would necessarily eliminate all marriage penalties and bonuses is the last one; however, that solution would violate the principle of treating all couples equally. The only other way to do away with all penalties and bonuses is to alter or eliminate the more than sixty provisions of the tax code that affect joint and single filers differently. This would be no small task and would most likely require fundamental tax reform.

The Bush plan would encourage charitable giving several ways:

- It would allow filers who do not itemize their deductions to claim a deduction for charitable giving;
- Individuals aged 59 or over could make tax-free contributions of IRA funds to charities; and
- Under current law corporations are allowed to contribute up to 10 percent of corporate income to charity. The Bush plan would raise this limit to 15 percent.

TABLE 14.2
Lessening the Marriage Penalty

Comparing the Marriage Penalty Provision of the Bush Plan
to HR 4810, a Marriage Penalty Relief Bill Passed
by Congress but Vetoed by Pres. Clinton

	BUSH	H.R. 4810
Standard Deduction	NA	Raise the standard deduction for married couples by $1,400—to twice that of the standard deduction for a single filer.
Brackets	NA	Widen the 15% tax bracket for married couples so it includes twice the income of the single filers' 15% bracket.
EITC	NA	Raise the beginning and end points of EITC eligibility by $2,000 for married filers.
Nonrefundable Tax Credits	NA	Extend the current provision that permits personal nonrefundable tax credits to count against both the regular and the alternative minimum tax.
Child Credit	Raise the income cutoff on eligibility for per child credit from $110,000 to $200,000 for married couples.	NA
Deduction for Lower-Earning Spouse's Income	Allow married couples filing jointly to deduct 10% of the lower-earning spouse's income, up to an earnings limit of $30,000.	NA

TABLE 14.3

Lessening the Marriage Penalty

Examples of Marriage Penalty and Bonus
1999

	PAUL	LISA	FILING AS COUPLE
Income	$40,000	$40,000	$80,000
Less Personal Exemptions	($2,750)	($2,750)	($5,500)
Less Standard Exemption	($4,300)	($4,300)	($7,200)
Equals Taxable Income	$32,950	$32,950	$67,300
Amt. Taxed at 15%	$25,750	$25,750	$43,050
Amt. Taxed at 28%	$7,200	$7,200	$24,250
Total Tax Liability	$5,879	$5,879	$13,248
Marriage Penalty			$1,490

	BOB	MARY	FILING AS COUPLE
Income	$0	$80,000	$80,000
Less Personal Exemptions	($0)	($2,750)	($5,500)
Less Standard Exemption	($0)	($4,300)	($7,200)
Equals Taxable Income	$0	$72,950	$67,300
Amt. Taxed at 15%	$0	$25,750	$43,050
Amt. Taxed at 28%	$0	$36,700	$24,250
Amt. Taxed at 31%	$0	$10,500	NA
Total Tax Liability	$0	$17,394	$13,248
Marriage Bonus			$4,146

Source: Tax Foundation (202) 783-2760, e-mail the Tax Foundation at tf@taxfoundation.org, or write us at 1250 H Street, N.W., Suite 750, Washington, D.C. 20005.

Do You Get The Message?

You should now have a pretty good idea of how the new tax plan works. If you review the information and compare it with your tax status, you'll be able to plan better for a more financially secure future by putting aside those extra dollars. Test your knowledge. Answer True or False to each statement.

1. Americans began getting checks in the mail in the summer 2001 of up to $600 for individuals, $1,000 for single parents and $1,200 for couples.

2. The tax rebates reflected the first year of a new 10 percent income tax rate on the initial $6,000 of an individual's income, $12,000 for married couples.

3. The standard deduction for married couples will gradually grow beginning in 2005 so that it becomes twice that of single taxpayers.

4. Under current law, filers receive a $1,000 tax credit for each dependent child under 17 years of age.

5. In an ideal world, parents should put aside $225 to $488 per month from the time the child is born to have enough to manage all expenses.

6. Most people spend 40 percent to 50 percent of their incomes on fixed and flexible expenses and know exactly where the rest of the money goes.

7. When funds are automatically deducted from your paycheck, saving becomes forced.

8. If one parent stayed home while the kids were young, the couple might be able to catch up financially if that parent starts working again when kids are in school.

9. If you inherit money, up to $50,000 per parent can be invested as a lump sum in your child's name without triggering a gift tax. The money grows tax deferred and only the financial gains are taxed at the child's rate when withdrawn.

10. Under current law, two-income married couples with similar incomes often pay higher income taxes than they would if they were unmarried, filing single tax returns. The Bush plan would partially alleviate this so-called marriage penalty.

Key:

1. F	6. F
2. T	7. T
3. T	8. T
4. F	9. T
5. T	10. T

Chapter 15

START PLANNING NOW: YOUR MONEY-MANAGEMENT CHECKLIST

"I can't definitively tell you when to do something. But you'll know when that moment hits you. When it does, don't pass up the opportunity to act. Don't just say no. Waiting for the ideal time is the excuse of a procrastinator. Don't wait until you have convinced your-self that everything must be just so for you to get involved. Remember, it's not about perfection, it's about passion, it's about purpose."

—TAVIS SMILEY
Television and Radio Talk Show Host

Discuss the following money-management practices with your family. Check yourself, and think honestly about how you're doing right now! I have left space for your personal notes on how you're doing. Write down what you could do to get started on this aspect of your journey to financial security.

1. We have a filing system to keep track of household bills, payments, and financial records.
   Do it now: _____
   _____

2. We have a written list of financial goals with an estimated cost of each goal.
   Do it now: _____
   _____

3. We regularly set aside money to achieve specific goals.
   Do it now: _____
   _____

4. We have an emergency fund available to use if necessary for minor catastrophes that are not covered by insurance.
   Do it now: _____
   _____

5. We have a written plan to allocate income to meet expenses and to save for future goals.
   Do it now: _____
   _____

6. We review and revise the family financial plan periodically to meet changing financial goals and needs.
   Do it now: _____
   _____

7. We compare costs and services of bank checking accounts, knowing that charges and services can vary widely.
   Do it now: _____
   _____

8. We move money from bank savings into higher return investments when the account balance exceeds current needs.
   Do it now: _____

   _____

9. We avoid impulse buying because unplanned spending could sabotage financial plans. We avoid overspending for holidays and special events by setting gift-spending limits that are in line with family goals.
   Do it now: _____

   _____

10. When we have a cash-flow problem, we cut back on spending until expenses are in line with income.
    Do it now: _____

    _____

11. We use credit carefully and avoid interest charges when possible by paying off credit-card debt monthly.
    Do it now: _____

    _____

12. We save for mayor purchases when possible rather than using credit cards and paying 14–21 percent interest on borrowed money.
    Do it now: _____

    _____

13. We know what insurance protection our employer(s) provides, and we supplement that insurance where necessary.
    Do it now: _____

    _____

14. We compare insurance coverages and costs, and purchase only the needed insurance.
    Do it now: _____

    _____

15. We have our employer(s) withhold the right amount in taxes in order to avoid lost interest income on large tax refunds.
Do it now: _____

_____

16. We check out charities before making contributions from phone or door solicitations, knowing that many are frauds.
Do it now: _____

_____

17. We just say no to telemarketing investment deals, knowing that if it sounds too good to be true, it is usually fraudulent.
Do it now: _____

_____

18. We carefully consider the tax-advantaged saving and investment opportunities provided by our employer(s).
Do it now: _____

_____

19. We compare the health-insurance options available through our employer(s) and choose the best option for our needs.
Do it now: _____

_____

20. We read current personal finance articles and work to improve our knowledge of personal money management.
Do it now: _____

_____

Chapter 16

SET GOALS AND BE A WINNER: FIVE SUREFIRE STEPS

"We're in this thing to go all the way."
—REGINALD LEWIS
Entrepreneur

Will you spend all your money today or save part of it for future goals? It is definitely more fun to save when you have specific goals in mind. This chapter will help you identify your goals, income, and expenses in order to help you decide how much to save each month to reach any goal by a specific date.

STEP ONE: SET YOUR DESIRED GOALS

- List your most important short-term and long-term goals.
- Estimate the cost of each goal and when you expect to reach the goal.
- Record the amount of money you have already saved to meet this goal.
- Figure out how much money to save each month in order to reach the goal.

The following goal-setting forms will serve as a map in guiding you toward your desired financial goals. They are here to assist you in your planning. Feel free to use the formula over and over again for your actual desires.

Goal Planner (example)

GOAL	*House Down Payment*
Years You Can Wait to Obtain Goal	10 years
Goal Amount (today's dollars)	$20,000

Annual Inflation Rate	5.00%
Annual Investment Growth	10.00%
Present Savings to Invest	$0.00

GOAL PLAN SUMMARY

Future Cost of Goal	$32,578
Additional Capital Required	$32,578
Additional Lump Sum Required	$12,560
Monthly Saving Required	$ 163

Goal Planner #1

GOAL	*Car Down Payment*
Timeline to Obtain Goal	
Goal Amount (today's dollars)	$

Annual Inflation Rate	5%
Annual Investment Growth	10%
Present Savings to Invest	$

GOAL PLAN SUMMARY

Future Cost of Goal	$
Additional Capital Required	$
Additional Lump Sum Required	$
Monthly Saving Required	$

Goal Planner #2

GOAL	*Major Vacation Cost*
Timeline to Obtain Goal	
Goal Amount (today's dollars)	$

Annual Inflation Rate	5%
Annual Investment Growth	10%
Present Savings to Invest	$

GOAL PLAN SUMMARY

Future Cost of Goal	$
Additional Capital Required	$
Additional Lump Sum Required	$
Monthly Savings Required	$

Goal Planner #3

GOAL   *Child's College Education*

Years You Can Wait to Obtain Goal

Goal Amount (today's dollars) $

Annual Inflation Rate   5%

Annual Investment Growth   10%

Present Savings to Invest $

GOAL PLAN SUMMARY

Future Cost of Goal $

Additional Capital Required $

Additional Lump Sum Required $

Monthly Savings Required $

Goal Planner #4

GOAL	*Setting Extra $ Aside*
Time to Obtain Goal	
Goal Amount (today's dollars)	$

Annual Inflation Rate	5%
Annual Investment Growth	10%
Present Savings to Invest	$

GOAL PLAN SUMMARY

Future Cost of Goal	$
Additional Capital Required	$
Additional Lump Sum Required	$
Monthly Savings Required	$

Goal Planner #5

GOAL	*Purchase Wedding Ring*
Timeline to Obtain Goal	
Goal Amount (today's dollars)	$

Annual Inflation Rate	5%
Annual Investment Growth	10%
Present Savings to Invest	$

GOAL PLAN SUMMARY

Future Cost of Goal	$
Additional Capital Required	$
Additional Lump Sum Required	$
Monthly Savings Required	$

Goal Planner #6

GOAL	*Wedding Cost*
Timeline to Obtain Goal	
Goal Amount (today's dollars)	$

Annual Inflation Rate	5%
Annual Investment Growth	10%
Present Savings to Invest	$

GOAL PLAN SUMMARY

Future Cost of Goal	$
Additional Capital Required	$
Additional Lump Sum Required	$
Monthly Savings Required	$

Goal Planner #7

GOAL   *Reaching a Specific $ for Savings Account*

Timeline to Obtain Goal

Goal Amount (today's dollars) $

Annual Inflation Rate   5%

Annual Investment Growth   10%

Present Savings to Invest $

GOAL PLAN SUMMARY

Future Cost of Goal $

Additional Capital Required $

Additional Lump Sum Required $

Monthly Saving Required $

Goal Planner #8

GOAL	*Retirement Plan*	
Current Age		
Retirement Age		
Length of Retirement		Years
Annual Retirement Income Needs	$	

Annual Inflation Rate	5%	
Annual Investment Growth	10%	
Present Savings to Invest	$	

RETIREMENT PLAN SUMMARY

Projected Retirement Expenses	$
Additional Capital Required	$
Additional Lump Sum Required Today	$
Monthly Savings Required	$

Goal Planner #9

GOAL *Business Start Up*	
Years You Can Wait to Obtain Goal	years
Goal Amount (today's dollars)	$

Annual Inflation Rate	5%
Annual Investment Growth	10%
Present Savings to Invest	$

GOAL PLAN SUMMARY

Future Cost of Goal	$
Additional Capital Required	$
Additional Lump Sum Required	$
Monthly Savings Required	$

Goal Planner #10

GOAL	*Income Property Down Payment*	
Years You Can Wait to Obtain Goal		years
Goal Amount (today's dollars)	$	

Annual Inflation Rate	5%
Annual Investment Growth	10%
Present Savings to Invest	$

GOAL PLAN SUMMARY

Future Cost of Goal	$
Additional Capital Required	$
Additional Lump Sum Required	$
Monthly Savings Required	$

STEP TWO: ESTIMATE YOUR INCOME

	Month 1	Month 2	Month 3
Wages (after deductions)			
• Wage Earner 1			
• Wage Earner 2			
Social Security			
Gifts/Allowance			
Interest			
Dividends			
Retirement Payments			
Unemployment Payments			
Alimony/Child Support			
Disability Payments			
Annuity Payments			
Rents on Real Estate			
Other			
Monthly Totals:	$_____	$_____	$_____

STEP THREE: RECORD YOUR EXPENSES

	Month 1	Month 2	Month 3
HOUSING			
Rent or Mortgage			
Electricity			
Gas/Oil			
Telephone			
Water/Sewer			
Property Tax			
Furnishings/Equipment			
FOOD/CLOTHING			
Food at Home			
Food away from Home			
Clothing			
Laundry/Cleaning			

	Month 1	Month 2	Month 3
TRANSPORTATION			
Bus, Train, Taxi			
Gasoline and Oil			
Auto Maintenance			
Parking/Tolls			
License			
LOANS			
Auto Loans			
Student Loans			
Other Loans			
INSURANCE			
Life			
Medical/Dental			
Auto			
Disability			
Homeowners/Renters			
EDUCATION AND PLAY			
Tuition and Books			
Subscriptions/Dues			
Recreation/Cable TV			
Vacations			
HEALTH CARE			
Doctors			
Dentist			
Medicines			
SET-ASIDES			
Emergency Fund			
Savings for Goals			
OTHER			
Personal Care			
Child Care			
Pet Food and Care			
Allowances			
Gifts			
Contributions			
Monthly Totals:	$_____	$_____	$_____

STEP FOUR: MATCH YOUR INCOME AND EXPENSES

	Month 1	*Month 2*	*Month 3*
Income	_____	_____	_____
Expenses	_____	_____	_____
Surplus or Deficit	_____	_____	_____

If Expenses Exceed Income
- Where are you overspending?
- Where can you cut back?
- Which expenditures can be postponed?
- How can you increase income?
  - A better job
  - A second job

If Income Exceeds Expenses
- Increase savings for future goals.
- Satisfy more immediate wants.
- Increase giving.

STEP FIVE: TRACK YOUR GIFT EXPENDITURES

Gifts are among those extra expenses that when added together can throw a budget way out of line. People tend to buy gifts on impulse and fail to comparison shop.

1. Place a total dollar amount by each category of gift spending last year.
2. Analyze last year's gift spending and estimate how much you will spend this year.
3. Decide whether you will spend more or less on gifts this year than last year.

	Spent on gifts last year	*Plan to spend this year*
Birthdays	$_____	$_____
Anniversaries	_____	_____
Weddings	_____	_____
Births	_____	_____
Deaths	_____	_____
Valentine's Day	_____	_____

	Spent on gifts last year	Plan to spend this year
Easter	_____	_____
Mother's Day	_____	_____
Father's Day	_____	_____
Graduation	_____	_____
Christmas & Hanukkah	_____	_____
Other	_____	_____
Total	$_____	$_____

Now that you've come this far, let's see how much knowledge and information you have gained to better your financial situation.

Match Terms

Match each of the terms listed below with the numbered definition. Write the letter in the space provided.

A. value   G. emergency fund

B. goal   H. insurance

C. decision making   I. budget

D. pay yourself first J. financial plan

E. net worth   K. college education

F. living expenses   L. investments

1. _____ money that is readily available for unexpected expenses

2. _____ example of a typical long-term goal

3. _____ something that a person considers to be important

4. _____ an organized process of allocating income to achieve financial goals

5. _____ what you own minus what you owe

6. _____ a specific statement about a desired future condition

7. _____ the idea that one should regularly set aside money for savings

Multiple Choice

Circle the letter which best completes the sentence.

1. Financial net worth is
   A. liquid assets minus long-term investments
   B. total assets minus total liabilities
   C. total investments minus total debt
   D. original securities price minus market value

2. "Pay yourself first" suggests that a person should
   A. avoid creditors and purchase nonessentials
   B. establish a business and work as president
   C. set aside money for regular savings
   D. pay back a loan you borrowed from yourself
   E. cut back on spending for essentials

3. Before investing, a person should have all of the following **except**
   A. a savings account equal to two years' income
   B. sufficient income to exceed current needs
   C. savings to cover typical emergencies
   D. adequate auto and property insurance
   E. adequate life and health insurance

Tom and Netta Worth have applied for a loan. In order to process their application, the bank needs to have the Worths' balance sheet, or net worth statement. Following is a list of their financial details:

$500 in checking	2 cars worth a total of $6,500
$850 in unpaid bills	stocks and bonds worth $12,000
$2,500 in car loans	house valued at $58,000
$18,000 house mortgage	personal property valued at $10,000

4. What is the amount of the Worths' total assets?

A. $87,000

B. $83,000

C. $37,000

D. $33,000

5. What is Tom and Netta's net worth?

A. $15,650

B. $11,650

C. $61,650

D. $65,650

True or False

Read each statement carefully and mark in the blank a **T** for True or **F** for False.

1. _____ People who have low incomes have little need to develop a personal financial plan.

2. _____ Personal money management is easy; people rarely need to spend time and effort learning how to manage money.

3. _____ People have a given set of financial values that remain with them for life.

4. _____ A financial plan can help eliminate uncertainty and conflict about financial matters.

5. _____ Investing should be the first priority in any financial plan.

6. _____ Your educational level is an important indicator of your expected lifetime earnings.

7. _____ It is against the law for employers to contribute to employee savings/investment programs.

Key:

1. G   4. J   6. B

2. K   5. E   7. D

3. B

Multiple Choice

1. B   3. A   5. D

2. C   4. A

True or False

1. F   4. T   6. F

2. F   5. F   7. F

3. F

Chapter 17

SUCCESS IS YOURS: TAKING IT TO THE TOP

"The only thing worse than failing is being afraid to try. Wait means never!"
—Reverend Martin Luther King, Jr.

At the beginning of this book you probably felt that learning to achieve financial success was an overwhelming task. Many African Americans assume they aren't capable of creating their own financial plan. By now you know that the "rules of the game" are available to everyone and the concepts aren't that difficult to learn. As you've seen chapter by chapter, the solution lies in learning one basic concept at a time and then implementing what you've learned. The key is to take one area at a time—assets, debts, and protection—and keep your eyes firmly focused on your goals, no matter what.

Dreams are only wishes. Solutions, on the other hand, are road maps that will lead to your peace of mind, your children's education, or comfortable retirement for you and your spouse. You may be tempted to hope for a miracle, but it's wiser to bet on a sure thing by following the proven principles that have already worked for the average American.

One thing remains—for you to place your blocks one by one. Based on the knowledge you've acquired, you will be surprised at how much progress you'll make. Cut your expenses whenever and wherever you can. Always look for the best value for your hard-earned money, and refuse to overpay. Look for ways to free up money to invest, and then let time work for you.

THIS IS ONLY THE BEGINNING

Now you have a foundation on which you can begin to build a plan that will handle everything. It can help send your children to college. It can help buy you a home or a new car, saving wisely and building an economic future that will safeguard you and your family. The stage is set, and it awaits your active participation in all the decisions that will influence and change your life.

There's nothing left for you to do but take control of your life and become financially empowered. Now that you're at the end of this book, I want to congratulate you for taking a stand for what's fair and right for you and your family. I congratulate you for deciding to stop being a victim and taking hold of your economic future. Thank you for committing to success. God bless you, and may life hold enormous rewards for you and your family. I'll look forward to hearing from you.

—JESSE B. BROWN
President, Krystal Investment Management

Glossary

AVERAGING (DOLLAR COST AVERAGING)

A system of buying securities at regular intervals with a fixed dollar amount. Under this system, investors buy by the dollars' worth rather than by the number of shares. If each investment is of the same number of dollars, payments buy more shares when the price is low and fewer when it rises. Thus, temporary downswings in price benefit investors if they continue periodic purchases in both good times and bad, and the price at which the shares are sold is more than their average cost.

BACK-END LOAD

The redemption charge an investor pays when making a monetary withdrawal. It is usually associated with fund redemptions.

BALANCED MUTUAL FUNDS

A fund that buys common stock, preferred stock, and bonds in an effort to obtain a higher return in a lower risk strategy. It typically offers a higher yield than a pure stock fund and generally performs better when stocks are falling. However, in a rising market the balanced fund usually does not keep pace with a pure stock fund.

BEAR MARKET

A term used to describe the fact that securities generally are declining. Usually lasting at least six months and normally not more than 18 months; caused by a strong conviction that a weak economy will produce depressed corporate profits.

BETA

Measures the volatility of an asset relative to the market.

BLUE CHIP STOCKS

A company known nationally for the quality and wide acceptance of its products or services, and for its ability to make money and pay dividends. Stocks of highly regarded, established corporations such as General Motors, IBM, and Xerox.

BOND

A contract between a borrower and a lender in which the borrower promises to pay a specified rate of interest for each period the bond is outstanding and repay the principal at the maturity date. Also called a "debt security." It is usually issued by government agencies, municipalities, and corporations.

BROKER-DEALER

A firm or individual acting as both a principal and an agent. A broker acts on behalf of the client searching for the best deal in the marketplace. A dealer acts on behalf of itself in making the market. The dealer actually buys and sells and maintains inventories of securities. A broker carries out the transaction but does not take possession of the security or maintain inventories.

BULL MARKET

A rising stock market over a prolonged period, usually lasting at least six months and normally not more than 18 months. Usually caused by a conviction that a strong economy will produce increased corporate profits.

CAPITAL GAIN

A capital gain arises when an investment is sold at a higher price than originally paid. In a mutual fund, capital gains are created when the fund buys and sells securities. These gains are then distributed to unit holders at least annually. Unit holders can also earn capital gains by redeeming their units at higher prices than they originally paid. The distribution is the realized gain on the sale of capital assets paid out to the shareholders.

CERTIFICATE OF DEPOSIT (CD)

A money-market instrument issued by a commercial bank. It promises to pay principal and fixed rate of interest at maturity, normally one year or less. The CD is characterized by its set date of maturity, interest rate, and wide acceptance among investors, companies, and institutions as a highly negotiable short-term investment vehicle.

CHURNING

Excessive trading in an investor's account, the sole purpose of which is usually to benefit the broker in the form of commissions. If the pattern of activity is inappropriate or inconsistent with the client's needs and objectives, or there are a volume of buys and sells for no suitable business reason, and if the prime result of such trading is the generation of commissions, then the practice is illegal under both SEC and exchange regulations.

CLASS OF SHARES

Shares issued by the same company having different rights or powers. For example, Class A shares may be voting shares, whereas Class B shares are not. In the case of mutual funds, different classes are structured to provide for various forms of sales charges. For example, Class A shares may contain a front-end sales load, whereas Class B shares may contain deferred sales charges along with 12b-1 charges.

COMMISSION

The broker's basic fee for purchasing or selling securities or property as an agent.

COMMON STOCK

A security representing ownership in a company. Stockholders actually own part of the corporate assets and so share in the profits and losses. Voting shareholders have the right to attend annual meetings and voice opinions on the general operations. Many shareholders have the right to elect the board of directors, and vote on important changes within the organization. Many companies pay annual dividends. Bondholders, on the other hand, are simply creditors with no ownership privileges.

CONTINGENT DEFERRED SALES CHARGE (CDSC)

A fee often charged when shares are redeemed during the first few years of ownership. Check the prospectus for details.

DISCOUNT BROKER

A brokerage house that executes orders to buy and sell securities at commission rates sharply lower than those charged by a full-service broker.

DIVERSIFICATION

The allocation of investment assets within an asset class, among different asset classes such as bonds, stocks, and real estate, or among geographical areas, to reduce risk.

DOW JONES

A reputable financial information services company. The Dow Jones Industrial Average (DJIA) and the Dow Jones Transportation Average (DJTA) are two of several indexes monitored daily by financial experts as overall indicators of stock market performance. The Down Jones Theory implies that a new market trend cannot be confirmed unless both indexes reach new highs or lows. The Dow Jones Transportation Average is a key U.S. market indicator, the weighted average price of thirty blue chip U.S. stocks listed on the New York Stock Exchange.

FAMILY OF FUNDS

A group of various funds sponsored by one issuer. Each fund has its own investment objectives.

FRONT-END LOAD

A sales charge applied to an investment at the time of initial purchase.

GROWTH STOCKS

Stocks that are expected to experience in the future a substantial growth in earnings per share and price while retaining a high proportion of earnings.

IRA ROLLOVER

Provision of the IRA law that enables persons receiving lump-sum payments from their company's pension or profit-sharing plan because of retirement or other termination of employment to roll over the amount into an IRA investment plan within 60 days.

INCOME STOCK

Stock paying high and regular dividends to shareholders.

INDIVIDUAL RETIREMENT ACCOUNT (IRA)

A personal, tax-deferred retirement account in which an employed person can deposit up to $2,000 per year.

INFLATION

Increases in the general price level of goods and services; i.e., your dollar won't buy as much as it used to. Inflation is commonly reported using the Consumer Price Index (CPI) as a measure. Inflation is one of the major risks to investors over the long term, as savings may actually buy less in the future if they are not invested with inflation as a consideration.

LOAD

Term used in the mutual-fund industry to identify the sales charge or commission on a particular fund. Common types of loads are front-end loads, or back-end loads (deferred sales charges).

MONEY-MARKET INSTRUMENTS

Debt instruments such as treasury bills or corporate paper with a maturity of less than one year, which are easily converted to cash.

MUNICIPAL BOND

A debt instrument issued by a state or local government. The interest is exempt from federal income taxation and also from federal and local tax in the issuing state. There are generally two types: general obligation (GO) and revenue bonds. GOs are backed by the full faith and credit of the taxing power of the issuer, and revenues are backed by the particular revenues or incomes from the project.

MUTUAL FUND

A regulated investment company that pools money and invests in various assets. There are many types, such as growth funds, income funds, bond funds, etc., all designed for a specific objective. Open-end mutual funds are fairly liquid in that investments and redemption transactions occur on a daily basis at net asset value.

NATIONAL ASSOCIATION OF SECURITIES DEALERS, INC. (NASD)

A self-regulatory organization (SRO) operating under the supervision of the SEC. Its purpose is to standardize practices, establish high ethical standards, and enforce fair and equitable rules.

NET ASSET VALUE (NAV)

Total assets less intangible assets less all liabilities divided by number of shares outstanding. In mutual funds, it is known as the bid price, or NAV.

NO-LOAD FUND

A mutual fund operated by an open end investment company that does not assess a sales charge. Shares are purchased directly from the fund, and not sold through a broker as is normal in a load fund.

PORTFOLIO

A collection of investments owned by an investor, an institution, or a mutual fund.

PROSPECTUS

A document that describes the financial details about a new issue and is required to be distributed to all investors prior to or at the time of the initial investment. Open-end mutual fund companies must send one to each new investor because the fund continually issues new securities.

RECESSION

Two consecutive quarters with a decrease in economic output.

RISK

The possibility that an investment will not perform as anticipated. An acceptable degree of risk must be determined by the individual with the understanding that the higher the expected return, the greater the risk factor. There are many different kinds of risk, such as exchange, inflation, interest rate, liquidity, political, etc. Most investors are considered to be risk adverse. That is, they seek security over risk.

SALES CHARGE

Also known as sales load. It is the fee charged on an investment, and varies according to the fund and investment. The charge is added to the net asset value when determining the offering price.

SECURITIES INVESTOR PROTECTION CORPORATION (SIPC)

Nonprofit corporation, established by Congress under the Securities Investor Protection Act of 1970, that insures the securities and cash in the customer accounts of member brokerage firms against the failure of those firms.

SECURITIES AND EXCHANGE COMMISSION (SEC)

Federal agency created by the Securities Exchange Act of 1934 to administer that act and the Securities Act of 1933, formerly carried out by the Federal Trade Commission.

Simplified Employee Pension Plan (SEP)

Pension plan in which both the employee and the employer contribute to an individual retirement account.

Standard & Poor's 500 (S&P 500)

A benchmark of U.S. common stock performance, it includes 500 of the largest stocks (by market value) listed in the United States.

Stock

Ownership of a corporation represented by shares that are a claim on the corporation's earnings and assets.

Total Return

Total earnings, which is composed of dividends, capital gains distributions, and price appreciation.

Transaction Costs

Cost of buying or selling a security, which consists mainly of the brokerage commission, the dealer markdown or markup, or fee but also includes direct taxes, such as the SEC fee, any state-imposed transfer taxes, or other direct taxes.

Variable Annuity

A life-insurance contract whose value fluctuates with that of the underlying securities portfolio. It differs from fixed annuities in that the rate of return is not constant and so is not as vulnerable to inflation issues.

Volatility

Characteristic of a security, commodity, or market to rise or fall sharply in price within a short term period.

Withdrawal Plan

A program in which shareholders may receive periodic payments from the investment.

YIELD

The return on an investor's capital investment. For a bond the current yield is the coupon rate of interest divided by the purchase price. Yields on bonds are inversely related to bond prices. As the prices of bonds go up, the yield declines.

ZERO-COUPON BONDS

A debt security that pays no interest. It is sold at a deep discount from the face value. The buyer receives a rate of return in the form of gradual price appreciation An example would be STRIPS, CATS, TIGERS, etc.

Index

Disclaimers

This book is designed to provide information in regard to the subject matter covered. It is sold with the understanding that the publisher and author are not engaged in rendering legal, accounting, or other professional services. If legal or other expert assistance is required, the services of a competent professional should be sought.

It is not the purpose of this manual to reprint all the information that is otherwise available to the author and/or publisher, but to complement, amplify and supplement other texts. You are urged to read all the available material, learn as much as possible about investing, and tailor the information to your individual needs. For more information, see the many references in the library.

Pay Yourself First is not a get-rich-quick scheme. Anyone who decides to invest must expect to invest a lot of time and effort. For many people, investing is more lucrative than other ways of making retirement income. Every effort has been made to make this book as complete and as accurate as possible. However, there may be mistakes both typographical and in content. Therefore, this text should be used only as a general guide and not as the ultimate source of investment advice. Furthermore, this book contains information on investing only up to the date of printing and predicts nothing for the future—it talks only about past performance.

Reference: FR1997-1024-007, review letter NASD: In accordance with Rule 2210(d) (2) (D) of the Association's Rules, since the cover of this book includes testimonials regarding the quality of Jesse B. Brown's investment advice, it must be made clear that the testimonials may not be representative of the experience of clients. The testimonials are not indicative of future performance or success, and no fee nominal or otherwise was paid for these testimonials. All testimonials concerning a technical aspect of investing were made by a person making the testimonial with the knowledge and experience to form a valid opinion.

In accordance with rule 2210 (f)(2)(a) and rule 2210 (f)(2)(d), Brown is a registered representative and General Principal of the NASD firm NPC Securities, Inc.

The purpose of this book is to educate and stimulate interest in the benefits of investing. The author and publisher shall have neither liability nor responsibility to any person or entity with respect to any loss or damage caused, or alleged to be caused, directly or indirectly, by the information contained in this book.

191

Jesse B. Brown is president of Krystal Investment Management, a financial advisory firm in Chicago. For a free copy of his monthly electronic newsletter, contact him at 1-800-541-9578 or 70 West Madison, Suite 1401, Three First Nation Plaza, Chicago, IL 60602. He is the best-selling author of the book *Investing in the Dream: Wealth Building Strategies of African-Americans Seeking Financial Freedom* and also produces audiotapes and other educational materials. Jesse B. Brown is available for lectures and keynote presentations. E-mail: krystal@Enteract.com; Web site, www.InvestInTheDream.com.